FRANK J. ZAMBONI & CO.
15714 COLORADO AVE. - PARAMOUNT
D0468068

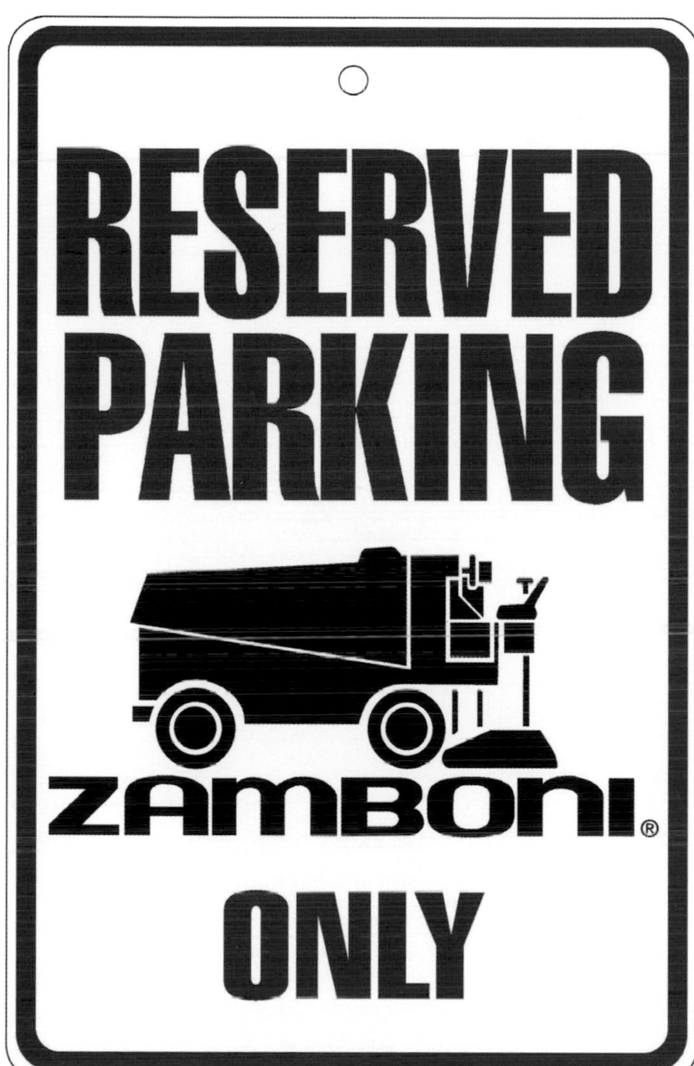
RESERVED
PARKING
ZAMBONI®
ONLY

5x7
ZAMB

ZAMBONI®

The Coolest Machines on Ice

ERIC DREGNI

Voyageur Press

First published in 2006 by MBI Publishing Company LLC and Voyageur Press, an imprint of MBI Publishing Company, Galtier Plaza, Suite 200, 380 Jackson Street, St. Paul, MN 55101-3885 USA

Library of Congress Cataloging-in-Publication Data

Dregni, Eric, 1968-
Zamboni : the coolest machines on ice / Eric Dregni.
p. cm.
Includes index.
ISBN-13: 978-0-7603-2439-4 (hardcover)
ISBN-10: 0-7603-2439-5 (hardcover)
1. Zambonis (Trademark) 2. Skating rinks--Equipment and supplies.
I. Title.
GV852.D74 2006
688.7'691--dc22

2006010914

Editor: Dennis Pernu
Designer: Tom Heffron

Printed in China

Contents

June 23, 1953 F. J. ZAMBONI 2,642,679

ICE RINK RESURFACING MACHINE

Filed May 16, 1949 4 Sheets-Sheet 4

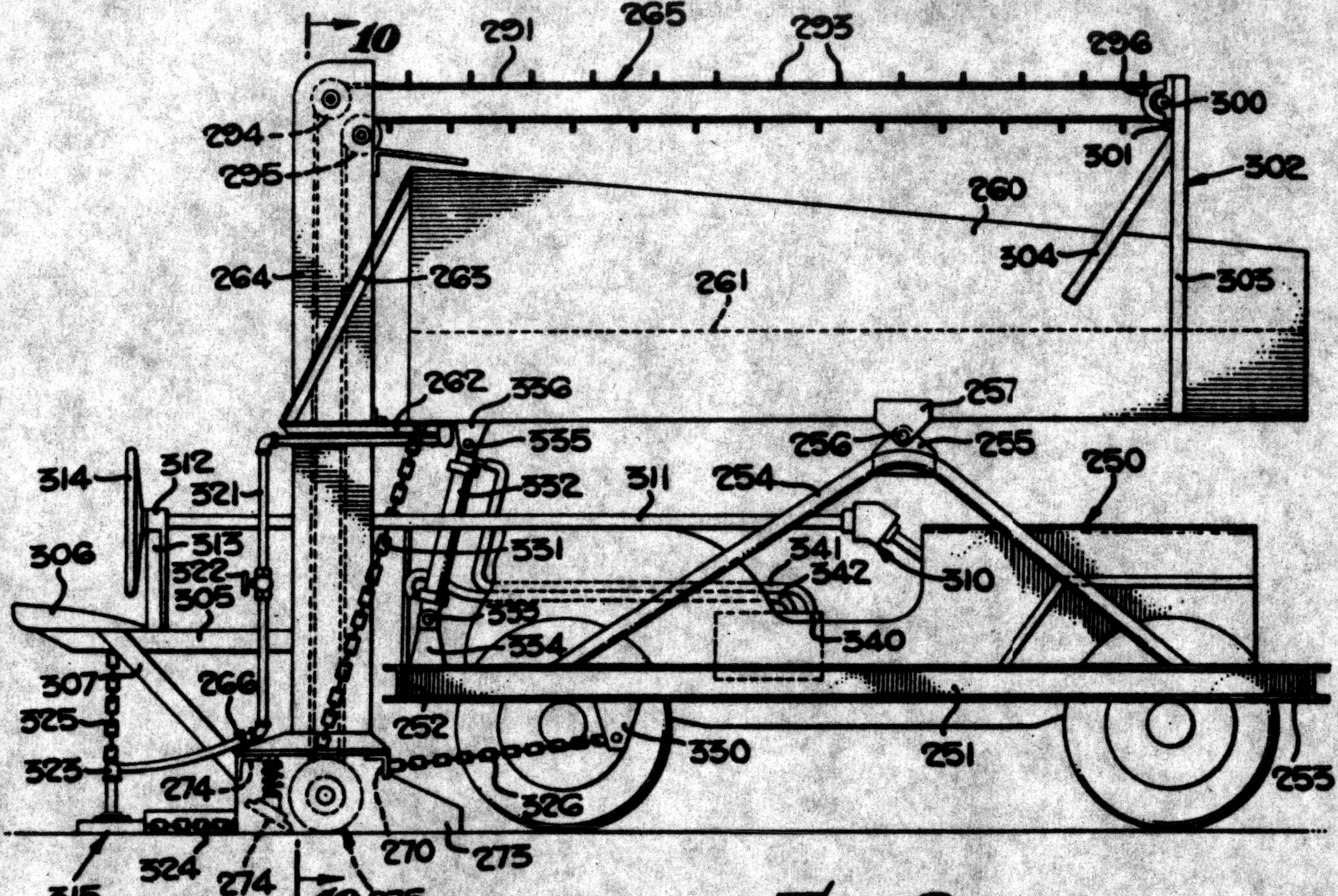

FIG. 9.

Acknowledgments

Walt Bruley, Michael Dregni at Voyageur Press, Hans Eisenbeis, Dan Falbo, Amanda Ferguson, Jim Fisher, Roger Godin at the Minnesota Wild, Goldy Gopher, Tim Mann, Brian McCarthy, Cheryl McCarthy, PK McCarthy, Dorothy Molstad and Dennis Pernu at Voyageur Press, Luther Rochester for clues on Zambonis as musical instruments, Dan Russell, Tom Sersha at the United States Hockey Hall of Fame, the Zellar brothers, and, of course, Richard Zamboni.

Introduction

In search of the birthplace of the Zamboni ice-resurfacing machine, I assumed I'd need to bundle up in my mittens and muffler and head to an igloo on the tundra. I was shocked to discover that Zamboni wasn't invented in the back of a machine shop on some windswept tundra. The home of this icon of ice skating isn't in the frozen northland (although a Zamboni assembly plant is located outside of Toronto). To see where Frank Zamboni dreamed up his world-famous ice resurfacer, I put on my shorts and sunglasses and flew to sunny Paramount, California, just south of Los Angeles. What? Zambonis are from Southern California?

I double-checked the address because all I found were warehouse buildings along a bumpy little side street of Paramount. Where was this Wonka Factory of the winter-loving world? Ice-resurfacing's Emerald City of Oz? Given the huge popularity of ice hockey and figure skating in recent years, I half expected to see lines of hardcore fans, toothless hockey players, and Michelle Kwan banging on some gilded gate to get a peek at the fabled machines and the people who make them. But the streets were empty and the buildings were all nondescript industrial spreads. Then I noticed a couple of young workers dangling chunky blue

Frank J. Zamboni

The man who started it all and proved the maxim "Necessity is the mother of all invention."

Anyone for a Snowball Fight?

Bert Nyenhuis tests a Model F ice resurfacer—and makes the Joneses green with envy that he can have a white Christmas in Southern California.

Ready to Roll

Richard Zamboni poses outside the Paramount, California, factory next to a new Zamboni ice resurfacer that will be sent halfway around the world.

and white metal slabs on hooks to dry the fresh paint. Around the corner on the sidewalk the sun beamed down on three shiny, partially assembled Zamboni machines that were lined up and slated to be shipped to China, Austria, and Nebraska upon completion. I'd found it at last.

Zamboni ice resurfacers are created one by one in the midst of movie stars and palm trees rather than hockey rinks and snow banks. Company President Richard Zamboni seems happy to have the factory in the relative obscurity of Los Angeles and enjoys test driving them at his Iceland Skating Rink.

I returned home from my visit, laden with piles of company literature and brochures. The next day, my computer crashed, so I brought it into my local computer shop, begging them to save the interviews I conducted at the Zamboni plant. The college student in front of me in line was getting her laptop repaired as well. When the tech guy at the counter asked her password to start her computer, she looked around and replied shyly, "Zamboni." Everyone in the store laughed as she blushed. I was stunned by the coincidence.

What is it about these chunky machines with the funny name that strikes a chord with skating fans? Students at Michigan Tech University formed a Zamboni Fan Club and proclaimed an annual "Zamboni Day." When racehorses Sweeping Beauty and Icecapade produced a little one, the new horse was lovingly named Zamboni. The name rolls off the tongue like the noises produced by the chunky, churning machines themselves.

Not everyone can agree on the best hockey team or the most graceful figure skater, but fans in every arena join together in their love for the Zamboni ice resurfacer. This book is the story of that machine, from its birth next to a rhubarb refrigeration plant in Southern California to the work it now performs around the globe.

A

First Period

The Birth of Zamboni

Frank Zamboni was born in Eureka, Utah, in 1901 and grew up on a farm in Idaho. He was pulled from school after the ninth grade by his immigrant father, Francesco, so he could help on the family farm and work as a mechanic in a local garage. In 1920, Frank and his brother, Lawrence, moved to Hynes-Clearwater, which would later become unified as the City of Paramount, California. Frank saved his money to study electricity at a trade school in Chicago and formed Zamboni Brothers Electric with Lawrence after graduating. They opened a refrigeration plant in 1927 to make block ice for old-fashioned iceboxes and to cool local farmers' fresh produce, such as carrots

Original Zamboni

The first Zamboni ice resurfacer, the Model A, was a one-of-a-kind machine with an enormous wooden box on top to catch the snow. In spite of its top-heavy, crude look, the Model A worked beautifully. Frank Zamboni continued updating the machine until it achieved its current design. Frank's son, Richard, remembers, "My dad drove me crazy because he'd change the design each time we had a new machine."

Ice
Skating
ICELAND

Iceland Skating Rink

When nearly every household in America wanted their own refrigerator, Frank Zamboni knew that his ice block business was doomed, so with his extra refrigeration equipment he rigged up an outdoor skating rink. The climate of Southern California proved not to be ideal for outdoor ice, so Frank covered the arena to make Iceland (left circa 1940, and below, circa 2006) in 1940 and began work on an ice resurfacer.

Scrape That Ice

Until Frank Zamboni revolutionized ice resurfacing, sharp planers were dragged behind tractors to shave off the top layer of ice. "It'll last forever," boasts this ad, because "It has very few parts." In other words, it was *too* simple.

and rhubarb, but soon refrigerators occupied nearly every kitchen across the country and the Zamboni brothers were left in the lurch.

Now possessing excess refrigeration capacity, Frank, Lawrence, and their cousin, Pete, saw an opportunity to put the ice-making machinery to a new use. Frank began testing outdoor ice surfaces on a lot adjacent to the plant, which led to the construction of an enormous, open-air ice rink. "Iceland" had a gala grand opening on January 3, 1940, and was one of the largest rinks in the country. However, the tropical sun and dry winds proved that Southern California was no place for outdoor skating.

continued on page 19

Prototype No. 3

Beginning in 1942, Frank Zamboni experimented with building an ice resurfacer, but his plans were foiled by the onset of World War II. In 1945, with the war over, Frank got back to work with access to military surplus parts. Prototype No. 3 combined the necessary operations to smooth the ice: shave, remove shavings to the tank, wash, and squeegee, but its two-wheel drive lacked traction on the ice.

Whence Zamboni? The Naming of the Machine

What's in a name? Wherefore art thou, Zamboni? When Frank Zamboni was looking for a name for his new factory, he wanted the grand-sounding "Paramount Engineering Company," which would have made his new invention the "Paramount Ice Resurfacer." Can you imagine hockey broadcasters announcing that mouthful? Fortunately, someone was already using the "Paramount Engineering" moniker, so he used his family name.

Fresh out of Utah, Frank Zamboni (second from left) and his brother Lawrence (far left) opened an electrical shop in Hynes-Clearwater, twin towns that later would be joined as Paramount under Frank's leadership as president of the local Kiwanis Club.

Ever since, writers have waxed poetic about this evocative name. The *Washington Post* extolled its virtues in 1997: "The name alone! Zamboni . . . one can imagine a family of trapeze artists, or the white smoke rising from the Vatican chimney as Cardinal Zamboni is named the next pope. Imagine the rare and treasured Zamboni cellos; the Zamboni opening in chess; the Count Zamboni who crashed at 178 mph in the Mille Miglia with the taste of Ava Gardner's kiss still on his lips; the Italian dirigible known as the Zamboni."

In Southern California, where the company is located, many people have never heard of Zamboni. Frank's son, Richard, seems a bit surprised at the celebrity of the family name and the reception he gets when he ventures north. People up there are surprised that it's a family name. Some ask him, "You don't have anything to do with that machine, do you?" or "You mean that's a family name?" Richard recalls someone who even asked, "Oh, so you're named after the machine?"

Richard continues, "Once I was up in Thief River Falls—way up there in northern Minnesota. Mike Mongoven, the city's director of parks and recreation, introduced me to some friends, saying, 'This is Richard Zamboni.'"

Thinking it a joke, a lady responded, "Oh, and I'm Julius Caesar." Once the person realized that Richard truly was of the Zamboni lineage, she was thrilled to meet him.

Tom Sersha, the executive director of the U.S. Hockey Hall of Fame in Eveleth, Minnesota, summed up the near-mythical status of the machine: "There's something about the name 'Zamboni.' People like it. They like to say it and hear it. It brings smiles to their faces."

Lounging on the Shovel

In the pre–Zamboni ice resurfacer days, a tractor first swooped by with a giant blade to scrape the top of the ice before a gang of shovelers scooped up the shavings.

Steaming the Ice

Some poor soul pulled a barrel full of boiling water behind the shovelers, leaving a smooth sheet of ice in time for the next hockey period. *Robert Wimmer*

Zamboni Model A

The first Zamboni ice resurfacer was restored by the factory in Paramount, California. Although it may look like a wooden crate on wheels, the Model A is fully functioning and resides in the Iceland Skating Rink. It is shown here both back in the day and during a more recent special appearance in Vancouver, British Columbia, with Richard Zamboni at the wheel (opposite).

continued from 14

"Iceland was covered in canvas and then they'd pull it off at night and we'd all go skating," recalls Frank's son, Richard. In May 1940, after five months of open-air skating, Iceland got a permanent roof.

Frank's pursuit of perfection would result in many improvements to the quality of ice-skating rinks everywhere. One of his earliest patents was for a rink floor that dispersed the cooling evenly below the ice, eliminating pipes that caused the surface to ripple.

Frank's innovation didn't stop with the ice surface. Since most visitors didn't have their own skates, Frank had "Zamboni Skates" made in Chicago especially for Iceland. The blades were trimmed down so the skater wasn't up so high, the

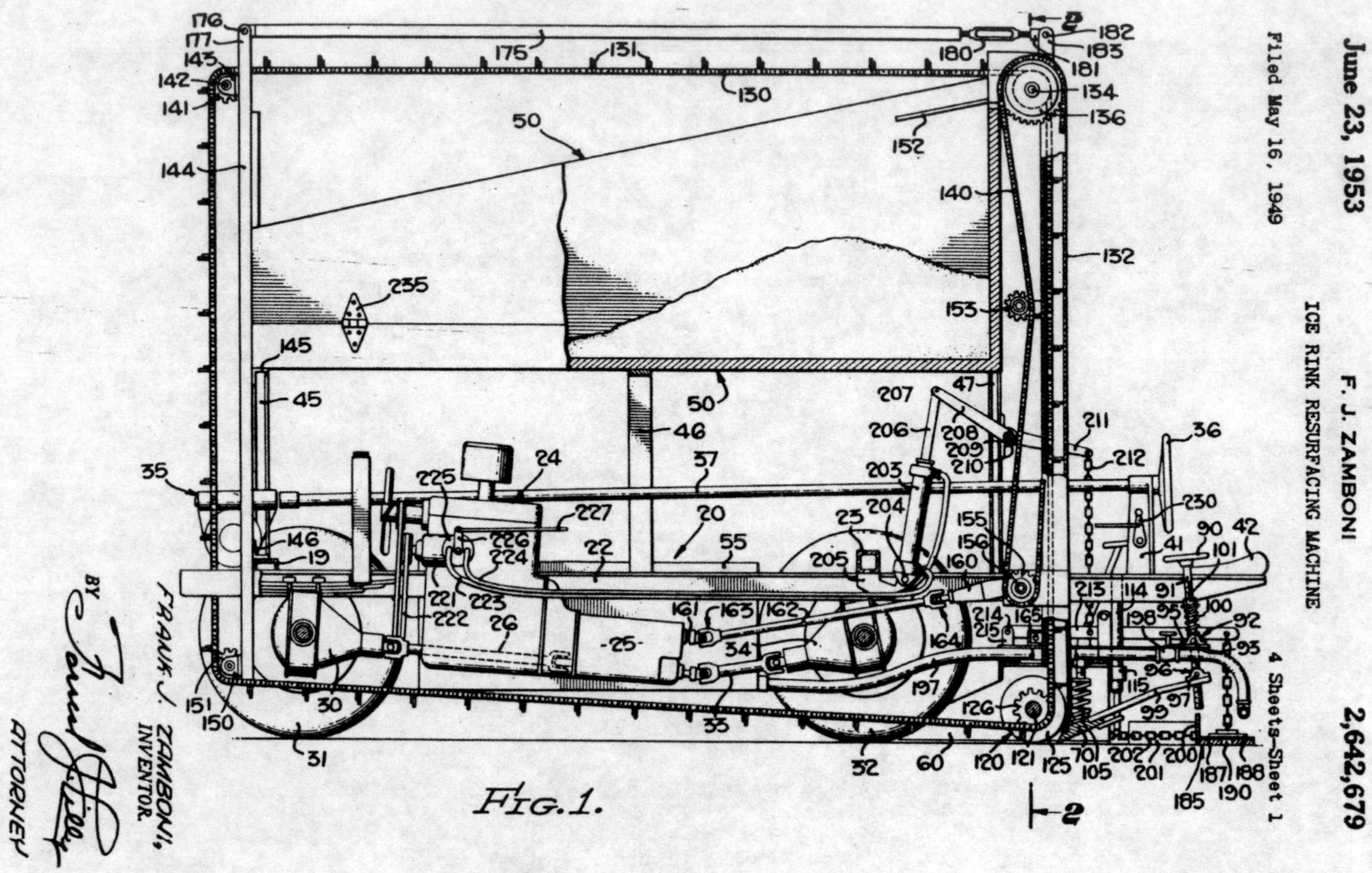

Zamboni Patent

In 1953, the U.S. Patent and Trademark Office finally granted Frank Zamboni bragging rights to having invented the very first ice resurfacer in the world: the Zamboni Model A.

theory being that a lower center of gravity made them less "tippy."

Even with these improvements, Frank soon realized that even the most devout skater would be hard-pressed to wait more than an hour for the ice to be resurfaced. Frank was fed up with the lengthy procedure that required a tractor to pull a planer that shaved the top layer of the ice, and three or four men with large scrapers to push the snow shavings into a pit. A hose was then used to squirt water across the ice surface, and squeegees pushed off the extra water containing dirt. After this washing operation, a light coat of water was sprayed on top for smoothness. "We could only make ice once a day. It would take them one-and-a-half hours to do it," Frank Zamboni told *USA Today* in 1985. There had to be a better way, and he was just the man to find it.

In March 1942, Frank rigged up a Ford-Ferguson tractor with a trailer to smooth down and scoop up the ice. His first attempt—a machine built onto a sled towed behind a tractor—

Ready for the Rest

Jeeps chassis were purchased from the Willys Corporation and built up into Zamboni ice resurfacers.

Zamboni Road Trip

When Sonja Henie ordered an ice resurfacer, Frank personally delivered his third machine. The only catch was that the Sonja Henie Ice Revue was performing in the Midwest. Frank loaded up the parts in a trailer and towed them in the Willys Jeep that would later become the body. During the frigid winter of 1950, he drove the machine from California to St. Louis, and then to Chicago.

neither smoothed the surface nor adequately picked up the shavings. Repeated experiments with the design proved fruitless. However, with World War II underway, ice-resurfacing was not a national priority.

After the war, military surplus provided cheap parts with which to create the world's first self-propelled ice resurfacer. In 1947, Frank began tinkering with axles from a Dodge army truck and other surplus parts. Frank ripped chassis rails from an old oil rig and stripped a hydraulic cylinder from a Douglas bomber. His third prototype performed the essential tasks of ice-resurfacing, but the two-wheel drive left its wheels spinning on the ice. "He built it out in the backyard," Richard Zamboni recalls of that first ice resurfacer. "My dad told me, 'I never would have finished it if people hadn't told me I couldn't do it.' He was a dedicated smoker, and he'd go out there and just look at the machine while smoking a cigarette."

Finally, on May 16, 1949, Frank's Model A was ready and the rink at Iceland was smooth as satin in record time. Frank applied for a patent on the machine, and Patent No. 2,642,679 was granted by the United States Patent and Trademark Office in 1953. Frank's broadest patent would protect his design for the next 17 years.

Frank now needed a name for his new invention and company. He decided on Paramount Engineering Company, the City of Paramount being home to his family, Iceland, and his ice resurfacer. To his chagrin, however, the name was already taken, so he named the machine after himself: Zamboni.

Soon, Frank built the second Zamboni ice resurfacer on a Jeep, dubbed the Model B and designated No. 1 (even though

No. 3

Sonja Henie bought two ice resurfacers from Frank Zamboni, who painted them fire-engine red because he knew that they'd be run in front of huge crowds at every one of Sonja's ice shows. Along with the Ice Capades, the exposure Henie's show provided eventually made Zamboni known throughout North America.

Model A was officially the first). In 1950, he sold it to the Pasadena Winter Garden for $5,000.

Then came Sonja Henie. When the Norwegian three-time Olympic medalist came to Iceland to practice with her traveling skating show, she fell in love with Frank's invention. Sonja begged him to build an ice resurfacer that she could take on the road with her "Hollywood" ice show. Richard remembers that his father was a bit surprised. "It really never was a money-making proposition for him in the beginning," Richard explains.

Accepting Sonja's order, Frank built his third Zamboni, another Jeep-based Model B. In the dead of winter, Frank personally drove the Jeep and a trailer full of parts to St. Louis, Missouri,

continued on page 29

The Burning Zamboni of Los Alamos

Zamboni No. 4 was delivered to the Ice Capades at Hollywood's Pan Pacific Auditorium in 1952. After being shipped with the show to Atlantic City, New Jersey, No. 4, a Model B, toured 22 cities across the nation with the Ice Capades. Bob Skrak skated with the show and then cleared the ice with the ice resurfacer, much to the amazement of crowds who'd never seen such a machine.

In 1953, the Ice Capades traded in No. 4 for a newer machine. A year later, No. 4 was ready to clear the ice at the new Iceland Skating Arena in Albuquerque, New Mexico (the original rink caught fire the year before).

In 1961, Bill Snelson, the owner of the Albuquerque rink, offered Model B No. 4 to the Los Alamos Skating Association along with all of his rink equipment for the paltry sum of $1,500. Soon, No. 4 was headed to the once-super-secret nuclear testing city of Los Alamos to keep the atomic scientists and their kids happy on their days off. The only condition to the sale was that the Los Alamos Skating Association had

Of all the Zamboni ice resurfacers, No. 4 has the most astounding history. After serving with the Ice Capades, it found its way to a rink in Los Alamos, New Mexico. After surviving a fire there—thanks to a brave Zamboni driver—it was restored and is now on display at the U.S. Hockey Hall of Fame in Eveleth, Minnesota.

to remove everything from the Albuquerque rink, including the Zamboni, by 6 p.m. the following Sunday. Building bombs would have to wait. All of the figure skaters and hockey players from Los Alamos piled into their cars and drove two hours down the Jemez Mountains into town. The caravan of skaters, led by a slow-moving Zamboni on a trailer, crept back up into the mountains at barely 20 miles (32 kilometers) per hour.

The oval rink high in the hills of Los Alamos measured 90 feet by 210 feet (27 meters by 64 meters) and was made by damming a creek to fill a small canyon at about 6,300 feet (1,920 meters) above sea level. The open-air rink relied on melted snow and the cold temperature of the high altitude.

In February 1973, the garage at the rink caught fire and the Los Alamos Fire Department was going to let old No. 4 go up in flames with it. But Zamboni driver Ted Dunn would not hear of it. He doused himself with water from a fireman's hose and barged into the burning building. Amid scorching flames, he threw a wet blanket over the machine and quickly tightened the battery terminals. He hopped in the saddle and revved the engine. At 9 miles (14.5 kilometers) per hour, he burst through the burning doors to safety. No. 4 was saved!

The firemen gathered around to admire the rescued Zamboni and the hockey team was pleasantly surprised to find that their sticks and gear had been stored in the snow tank and thus mostly survived the blaze.

The machine has since been lovingly restored by the Zamboni factory in Paramount, California, and placed on display at the U.S. Hockey Hall of Fame.

Ice Capades

When the Ice Capades saw Frank Zamboni's new ice-resurfacing contraption being used on Sonja Henie's traveling skating show, the former jumped on the bandwagon. How else could you assure that skating pirates, circus clowns, and the fabulous Donna Atwood wouldn't fall on their face because of bad ice?

Donna Atwood and Model E

Donna Atwood received her first pair of skates at age 13 and won the national women's singles and doubles championships within two years. When World War II left the Olympics on hiatus, Atwood had little choice but to turn pro at the age of sixteen. While Sonja Henie had her own traveling show, Atwood was a natural as the leading lady of the Ice Capades.

ICE CAPA
THE BRAND NEW PRESENTATION OF WALT DISNEY'S
Snow White and the Seven
ONE OF 10 GREAT
FOR EVERY KID
from 6 TO 106
ICE CAPADES
OF 1954
5000
Seats

Snow White and the Zamboni

When the Ice Capades came to Atlantic City in 1954, promoters placed their second Zamboni, the first Model E, in front of the theater on New Jersey's famous boardwalk. After Sonja Henie's show and the Ice Capades toured the country with their respective Zamboni ice resurfacers in tow in the early 1950s, sales of the machines climbed slowly. Between 1950 and 1953, 13 Zamboni ice resurfacers were built, each one an improvement on the previous one.

continued from page 23

where he hoped to meet Sonja's ice show and assemble her machine. Unfortunately, the performance in St. Louis had concluded and the show had moved on to Chicago, so Frank got back on the road to meet up with Henie. Sonja liked her Zamboni so much she bought a second machine for her overseas skating show.

Sonja's traveling show was the best publicity Zamboni could have asked for. The Model B was carted around the country to skating rinks that struggled with the same problems Iceland had overcome.

The Ice Capades show soon heard about this fabulous ice-resurfacing machine and became Zamboni's next customer. After watching Donna Atwood's spinning pirouettes, crowds were equally mesmerized between sets by this newfangled ice machine. Richard Zamboni credits this famous ice show with really spreading the word about his dad's invention. "[Operator and chief mechanic] Bob Skrak traveled around with the Ice Capades and showed off the machine," Richard explains. "This helped sell them." Interestingly, Skrak also happened to be a skater in the show. Today, No. 4 resides with the United States Hockey Hall of Fame.

Despite the success with Ice Capades, Frank Zamboni did not stop with his early designs. Fortunately, Frank ignored his contemporary naysayers and continued on his quest to perfect his ice resurfacer. "My dad drove me crazy because he'd continually change the design of the machine," Richard remembers. "He didn't get past the ninth grade and thought he was educationally

A Driver's Dream

What Zamboni driver wouldn't want lovely Donna Atwood to hop on the running boards? Driver Bob Skrak grips the wheel of Zamboni No. 4, the Model B that has since been fully restored.

Frank Zamboni Studies a Prototype

Frank Zamboni spent hours in the old workshop behind Iceland Skating Rink, contemplating how to perfect an ice-resurfacing machine.

Model D

Sold in 1953 to a traveling skating show, Model D No. 12 performed for years, but its fate is unknown.

challenged, but he was really a genius at design. I wasn't as mechanically inclined as my dad, but because I could draw a straight line and he couldn't, he relied on me to do parts drawings. "Each of the first dozen or so machines Frank built was an improvement on its predecessor. "My dad had been changing every machine up until 1954," Richard explains. Later reflection made it possible to classify the early machines according to their development and give them model designations.

Having refined the resurfacer greatly since completing the Model A, and noting increased acceptance of the machine around the country, Frank standardized the design in 1954 by producing 10 identical machines. He then undertook the challenge of selling them. This new design became the Model E and customers in 1954 included the Boston Garden, the Boston Arena, the Cleveland Skating Club, the Providence Arena, and Hershey Arena, among others. Frank sold and delivered 10 more of these units in 1955, bringing the number of Model E machines produced to 21.

Traction on the ice was a major problem with early models, even at slow speeds. Pointing to the wheels of a classic Model JR recently restored in the California Zamboni factory, Richard says, "We took the Jeep tires over to a tire recap shop and they scarfed off all the tread. Then we put walnut-shell recaps on them to make them grip to the ice."

The building blocks of the early Zamboni ice resurfacers were Willys Jeeps. The machines were built around the entire body and chassis, leaving a complete Jeep visible somewhere underneath all those storage tanks and snow-pushing paddles. With the introduction of the Model F, Frank used as a platform a stripped Jeep chassis bought from the Willys Corporation. The Model F was Frank Zamboni's second standardized design and was the industry standard from 1956 until 1963.

Holiday on Ice

The first Model F, No. 37, was sold to the St. Paul (Minnesota) Auditorium. Later, it operated at the Brown County Memorial Arena in Green Bay, Wisconsin, until its recent placement in the NHL Minnesota Wild's home arena, nearly 45 years after the machine was built.

The Model F was also the primary machine used during the 1960 Winter Olympic Games in Squaw Valley, California. The Zamboni machines used in Squaw Valley were the first mechanical ice resurfacers used at the Olympic Games. There were six Zamboni machines on site for the Games, including the first

First Model F

The earliest Zamboni ice resurfacers were mostly dismantled or forgotten in anonymous rubbish heaps. Only six of Zamboni No. 37's predecessors have been unearthed and restored. No. 37 was the first Model F and today it rests high on a ledge in the concourse at the Xcel Energy Center in downtown St. Paul, Minnesota, for all to see. ***Photo by Tracy Meister***

Model F

Bert Nyenhuis shows off a Model F ice-resurfacing machine with slick whitewalls that wouldn't have seemed out of place at the drive-in. Frank Zamboni's grandson, Frank, is peeking out from inside the machine.

electric-powered machine. The success of the Zamboni machines at that televised event introduced them to rink operators in Europe, Japan, and around the world, making possible their acceptance as the premiere method of maintaining quality ice.

Back at the factory, it became apparent that the Jeep chassis was a limitation to the machine's development. "The Jeep frame was too fragile and timid to dump the snow," Richard explains. By 1964, the Jeep was abandoned as the basis of the Zamboni, and

continued on page 38

Olympic Medals

Not until 1960 did Zamboni ice resurfacers make their Olympic debut. The Olympic Committee bought three custom-designed Zamboni machines for the 1960 Winter Olympics in Squaw Valley and leased three more. Frank Zamboni "designed machines especially for them," says his son, Richard. "People saw them when it was televised across the country and around the world."

One of the six machines was a bizarre three-wheeled affair that was easier to maneuver around the sharp turns of the hockey rinks. This experimental model was actually Zamboni's first electric-powered machine.

Zamboni ice-resurfacing machines became standard at the Winter Olympics. A Zamboni cleared the ice when the U.S. hockey team took the gold at the 1980 Olympics in Lake Placid. The ice resurfacers flew to the 1998 Olympics in Nagano, Japan. Twenty Zamboni machines were on hand to clear all of the ice surfaces at the 2002 Olympic Games in Salt Lake City. And the ice resurfacers hypnotized the crowds at the 2006 Olympics in Torino, Italy.

Zamboni ice resurfacers made their television debut at the 1960 Winter Olympics in Squaw Valley, California, and Frank Zamboni even had the foresight to match their paint schemes to the Olympic Village. A few years later, Frank reported proudly, "That was the first time the whole world got to see them on TV."

To make the sharp turns around the boards in ice arenas, Frank Zamboni designed a three-wheeled Zamboni ice resurfacer that was used at Blythe Arena during the 1960 Squaw Valley Winter Olympics.

Ever since its ice resurfacers appeared at the 1960 Winter Olympics in Squaw Valley, Zamboni has been an ubiquitous presence on the Olympic ice, as seen here at the 1998 games in Nagano, Japan. *David Klutho*

continued from page 35

the famous "rolling breadbox" look was introduced. A high-capacity vertical auger was developed and replaced the old paddle system as the means of conveying the snow to the storage tank.

Frank's next production effort, the Model HD, became the first production dumping machine and was an immediate hit with rink operators. The Model HD was built from 1964 to 1968 with a Wisconsin air-cooled engine, manual transmission, and a vertical auger conveyor. Several more models of the Zamboni ice resurfacer would be introduced to the world, including the Model JR, Model K, Model L, and Model HDB. Frank learned from each model and applied that knowledge to his continuous effort to improve upon his product. For the Zamboni JR model, the company even considered using the automatic clutch from Space Age Salsbury scooters, built in nearby Pomona. "We just didn't have enough speed on the Zamboni to shift it up," Richard remembers of the experiment. "It works fine on scooters, but not on a Zamboni."

In 1978, the standard-size Zamboni machine was completely redesigned, launching the 500 Series. The Zamboni 500 featured a liquid-cooled Volkswagen engine. Similar in appearance, but battery-powered, the Zamboni 550 came out the same year and became the world's first production electric ice resurfacer. While the 500 and 550 were being built in Paramount, production began in a Canadian Zamboni-manufacturing facility in Brantford, Ontario, in 1983.

The Zamboni 552 replaced the 550 and made its debut in 1990 with new state-of-the-art electronics. Emission-free, the revolutionary 552 was featured at the Winter Olympics in Lillehammer, Nagano, Salt Lake City, and Torino. In 2003, Zamboni further increased the power and efficiency of the 500 Series with the introduction of the Model 540, which features a 2.5-liter, 4-cylinder overhead-valve liquid-cooled 63-horsepower engine.

Today, Zamboni drivers recall the tiresome old days of smoothing down the ice by hand and give thanks for the countless hours saved, thanks to these boxy machines. "Before the Zamboni, they'd send six men out with shovels to clean the ice," Justine Townsend Smith of the Ice Skating Institute of America told *USA Today* in 1985. "Rinks would lose several hours in a day out of scheduling, and the ice was never good."

At the Duluth (Minnesota) Curling Club, which also hosted hockey games once upon a time, "They'd have to pray for cold

continued on page 45

Enter the Breadbox

By 1964, the limitations of the Jeep chassis had become apparent. Here, Frank pilots a three-wheeled prototype that tested rear-wheel steering.

Around the Oval

This Zamboni Model HDC was manufactured with a special cab for the driver to avoid frigid outside temperatures on giant outdoor speed-skating rinks.

ZAMBONI
GAS
FIRST CHOICE
FOR HEATING
MILWAUKEE'S HOMES

Alternative Fuel

In 1966, Zamboni made the Model L for outdoor rinks with a special cab for the driver. Although this enormous machine ran on gasoline, the advertisement on its side panels read, "Gas: First Choice for Heating Milwaukee's Homes," referring, of course, to natural gas.

Model M

Built from 1970 to 1976, the Zamboni Model M used the same paddle system to convey snow to the tank as the earliest Zamboni Model A. More popular models lifted the snow into the tank via giant augers.

Z

Early Resurfacing Contraption

This precursor to Frank Zamboni's machine filled the little trailer with water to be spread evenly across the ice. These early jalopies usually only did one part of the job that Frank Zamboni's miracle machines later accomplished: shaving the ice, collecting the snow, and leaving a film of hot water atop the ice. *Robert Wimmer*

Pre-Zamboni

Frank Zamboni wasn't the only one who dreamed of using surplus Jeeps from World War II to resurface ice. This machine, used at the Hobart Arena in Troy, Ohio, probably just shaved the ice and maybe gathered the shavings in the box behind the driver.

continued from page 38

weather, then they'd open up the windows and let all the cold air in," driver Walt Bruley recalls. "Then guys had to push a plow—like a snowplow on the front of a truck." A 55-gallon (208-liter) barrel on wheels with hot water was wheeled out. "At the end of the night, they'd bring a little tractor out to scrape the top of the ice and smooth it out. I threw up my hands and shouted, 'Somebody give me a sign! There has got to be a better way!'"

Zamboni saved the day.

While Frank Zamboni's Model A may not be as sleek as fellow Italian Enzo Ferrari's sports cars, the first resurfacer revolutionized hockey and figure skating. Even with this groundbreaking technology ingeniously assembled from a pile of spare parts, modern critics have lamented the lack of smooth lines. Canada's *The Expositor* newspaper in Brantford,

continued on page 48

Zamboni as a Part of Speech

The popularity of Zamboni ice resurfacers has landed them on the hallowed pages of *Webster's Dictionary*, in crossword puzzles, and on the answer side of a Trivial Pursuit card. A Zamboni solved a crime on *CSI* and ran over Carla's husband, Eddie, on an episode of *Cheers*.

The popularity of Zamboni ice resurfacers has also seen the word used as a noun (simply "a Zamboni") and a verb ("to Zamboni the ice"). But, as company CEO Richard Zamboni puts it, "It's good to be well-known. It's not good to be generic. The machine is not a 'Zamboni.' It is a Zamboni ice resurfacing machine."

Because of the popularity of Zamboni ice resurfacers, combined with being the first machine and having a strong presence in the ice-resurfacing market, the company is determined that its name not go the way of "Kleenex," "Frisbee," and "Jacuzzi." The Zamboni company has worked hard to keep their trademark under control and has even registered the shape of its machine as a federally registered trademark, like the Coca-Cola bottle and the grille on Jeeps. To address the proper use of their trademark, the Zamboni company Web site states:

A trademark is always an adjective. Never a noun. So when referring to ZAMBONI, please use it in the correct context. ZAMBONI is the brand, and ice resurfacing machine is the generic product name.

- **Zamboni® ice resurfacer**
- **Zamboni® ice resurfacing machine**
- **Zamboni® brand of apparel and accessories**

The machine is not "a Zamboni," it is a ZAMBONI ice resurfacing machine. The name must be capitalized and spelled correctly and should never even remotely be used in a generic sense. Never use

—World-Herald Photo.

The thingamajig . . . Skrak does work of 10 men.

Automation Keeps Ice Smooth for Show

Automation is here, as far as spectators at the Ice Capades of 1956 are concerned.

During intermission time at Ak-Sar-Ben Coliseum, skaters leave the ice and the "thingamajig" takes over.

The thingamajig is a jeep which performs a variety of jobs as it is driven around the ice-covered arena.

Its over-all function is to make the ice smooth again for the second half of the show.

A blade on the thingamajig scrapes the ice.

An auger-like attachment pushes the scrapings off the ice onto a conveyer.

The conveyer carries shavings to a receptacle at the top.

As the thingamajig moves along it leaves behind on the ice a coat of water, which fills cracks and freezes.

Robert Skrak, operator of the thingamajig, prepares the ice before and after e[illegible] show and during each ir[illegible] mission.

"It's a time-saver, [illegible] right," Mr. Skrak said.

The thingamajig is a[illegible] Capades property. The [illegible] seum, which doesn't h[illegible] thingamajig, depends [illegible] men to scrape, sweep [illegible] water the ice when the [illegible] is open to public ska[illegible] said Harry Fowler, Colis[illegible] manager.

Omaha

Before Frank Zamboni came up with the familiar "Zamboni" logo, journalists were left to their own devices to name the machine. When the Ice Capades came to Omaha, Nebraska, in 1956, a local newspaper wrote that "During intermission time at Ak-Sar-Ben Coliseum, skaters leave the ice and the 'thingamajig' takes over."

Mini Zamboni

The Zamboni Model 100 is perfect for light use on neighborhood rinks and ponds. The Zamboni company paints the ice-resurfacing trailer to match the John Deere tractor and sells the two as a unit.

continued from page 45

Ontario, judged that "The original Zamboni looks like the offspring of a field tractor and a warehouse crate." And another modern journalist complained that "The Zamboni Model A was a hideous, Rube Goldberg contraption with a wooden bin, a maze of pulleys and crude four-wheel drive."

Zamboni offers a wide range of ice resurfacers. The Model 100 is a small unit for ponds and parks, and is offered as a package with a John Deere garden tractor. "People wanted it to match the John Deere green," Richard explains. "It's a cute little thing; I love to drive it." The giant of the bunch is the Model 700 used on figure skating, hockey, and bandy rinks. Indeed, Frank Zamboni's belief in ongoing product improvement and innovation lives on in the company he founded.

The first Zamboni ice-resurfacing machine, the Model A, has been fully restored and stands on display in the Iceland Skating Rink in Paramount, California, next to a Model E34 that logged close to 50,000 miles (80,000 kilometers)—all on ice—over the course of 40 years of service.

Model E

The Willys Jeeps that were used to make early-model Zamboni ice resurfacers were clearly visible. The driver's seat was moved to the rear to allow more room to store the snow. This 1955 Model E from the early 1950s is believed to have been the first Zamboni machine delivered to a Canadian arena.

Frank told *USA Today* in 1985 that he was surprised when ice rinks across the country began requesting his early machines. "I had no idea it would be a business itself," he recounted. In spite of an education that ended in the ninth grade, Frank Zamboni was given an honorary doctorate in engineering in 1987 from Clarkson University in Potsdam, New York. He died a few months later.

Second Period

The Nature of the Beast

Driving the Zamboni may look like simply spinning circles on the ice, but the hazards are many. Walt Bruley, a self-described "Zamboni Man," resurfaces the Duluth Entertainment Convention Center ice on the "Waste Management Zamboni" painted to resemble a garbage truck. Bruley warns of the pitfalls of pucks, broken sticks, and items that fans throw on the ice, all of which can foul up the machine. "Every once in a while, the nails from the boards, which were made of plywood, would pop out with the puck bouncing around, and we'd puncture the tires on the Zamboni," Bruley remembers of his early driving days. "One guy cut his face on a nail—we call him Scarface."

In most areas, no driver's license is required to operate an ice resurfacer. Legally, almost anyone can drive a Zamboni. Doing it correctly, on the other hand, requires hours of practice. "Part of the deal when my dad sold them in the early fifties was we'd show them how to run them," Richard Zamboni says. Frank Zamboni

Climb Ev'ry Mountain

This Zamboni Model 500 shaves off about 1/32 of an inch (0.8 millimeters) of ice each time it passes.

Milestone Zamboni

Frank Zamboni and his wife, Norda, celebrate the completion of Zamboni No. 1,400 in front of the Paramount, California, offices in 1972.

Zamboni Guts

Company president Richard Zamboni shows off the interior of one of his machines on the factory floor in Paramount.

Zamboni Drives a Zamboni

Richard Zamboni maneuvers a new Zamboni machine through the factory. He often takes the new ice resurfacers over to the testing track a few blocks away at his Iceland Skating Rink in Paramount, California.

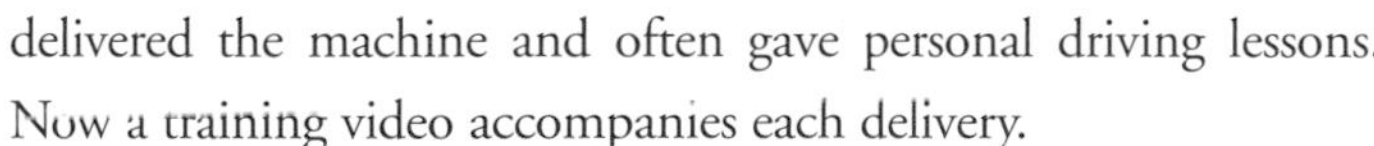

delivered the machine and often gave personal driving lessons. Now a training video accompanies each delivery.

"I could teach you how to drive it in a day, but it takes two to three years experience to master it," Bruley continues. "It's so unnatural because you can't see. You have this big massive thing in front of you and you're expected to hit a mark without being able to see it. I try not to get too happy out there because then you don't pay attention. Everyone waves and wants me to honk. Never get too happy—always pay attention."

Bruce Tharaldson, who drove the Zamboni at the since-demolished Met Center in Bloomington, Minnesota, told *Sports Illustrated*, "You'll see little kids waving at you. I try to make them feel good by waving back, but the first couple of times around the

View from the Chair

Imagine trying to cozy up to the boards but not actually bonk into them. The Zamboni driver relies on a sixth sense to smooth the ice perfectly. No pesky odometer or speedometer is necessary, but an hour meter adorns the dashboard.

"Never Get Too Happy"
With limited visibility and many handles to maneuver, Zamboni drivers need to ignore the cheers and jeers of the audience as they resurface the ice slick between periods. Jumpsuit optional.

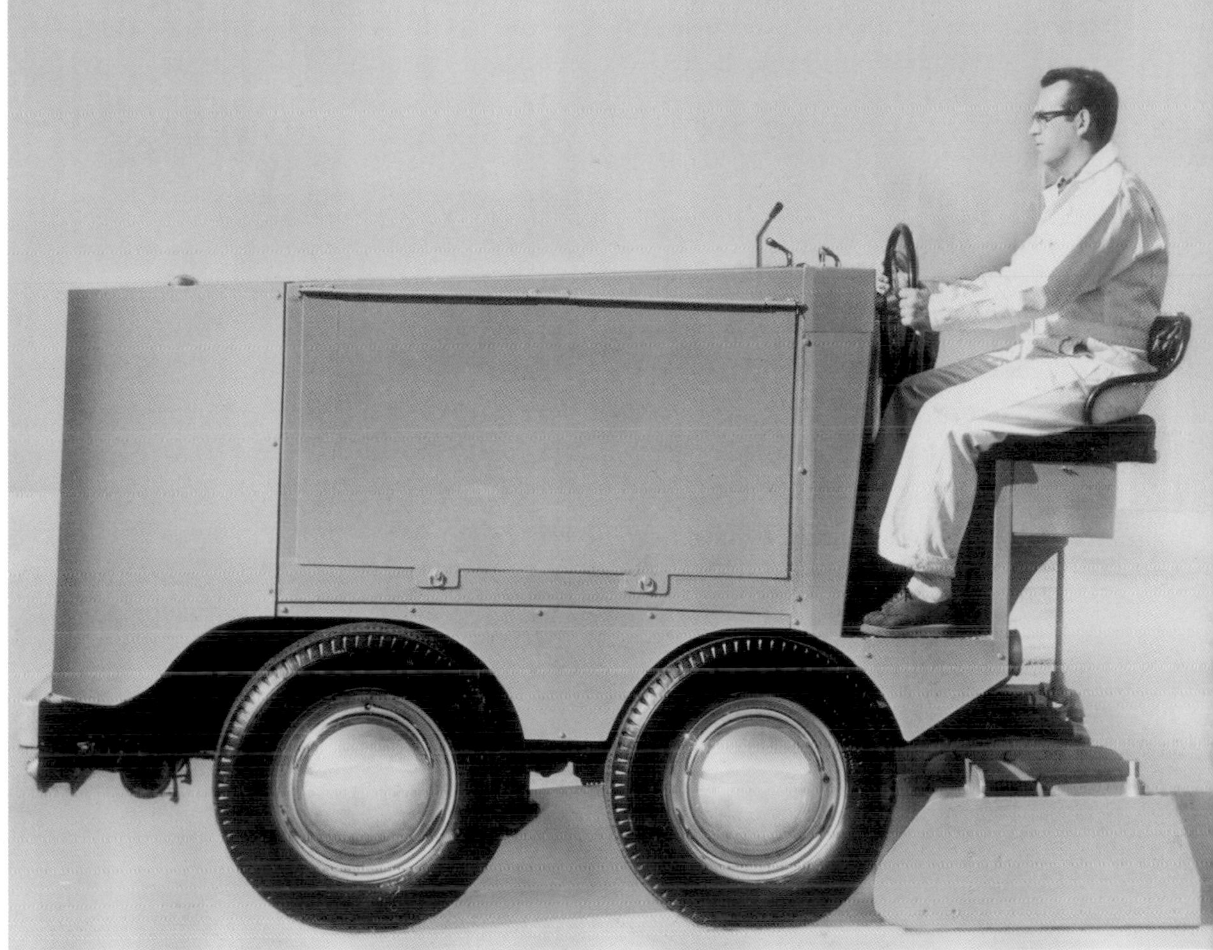

rink it's hard. . . . Don't do it right and you'll have a swamp. Or you'll dig in the surface and you'll have the officials down on their hands and knees trying to fix a hole. That's a Zamboni driver's nightmare."

To prove that resurfacing the ice is serious business, Bruley recalls a group of hockey fans in Section 26 who would heckle him at every game about his Zamboni driving. "A guy from the stands one night after the game came down and said, 'I've been watching you do that for 25 years. What do I have to do to become a Zamboni man?' We gave him a job and he slowly learned how to do it and couldn't believe how hard it is. He drives now, and he's armed with the stories when his buddies in Section 26 start jeering."

Richard Zamboni concedes that driving a Zamboni is a refined art. "Take it easy and keep up your momentum and you'll be fine," he explains. "But don't go too fast—it's a delicate balance." Then he adds, laughing, "I've put them through the boards myself a couple of times."

Richard also remembers that the NCAA contacted the Zamboni Company in 1957 regarding the turning radius of the machine. At that time, they recommended a 15-foot radius in the corners of the rink. However, because of increased usage of the machine and its inability to cover that tight of a turn, the NCAA changed the minimum radius in their *Ice Hockey Guide* (commonly referred to as the "Rule Book") to 20 feet, per the Zamboni Company's suggestion.

Zamboni Hypnosis

Hockey players scrapping for the puck and smashing into each other at breakneck speed require constant attention from fans straining to catch all the action from the edges of their seats. When the buzzer sounds to end the period, the crowd breathes a collective sigh of relief and the Zamboni ice resurfacer slowly comes out to clear the ice. Weary fans watch mesmerized as the blocky machine tick-tocks across the ice like a pendulum placing them under its spell.

"There are three things in life that people like to stare at: a flowing stream, a crackling fire, and a Zamboni clearing the ice," Charlie Brown famously pronounced.

In June 1998, *ESPN the Magazine* agreed with the round-headed *Peanuts* character: "Who hasn't basked in the hypnotic, between periods calm of the circling mechanical dervish and marveled as the elegant synergy of stainless-steel blade, churning screw and big squeegee lays down a perfect 1/16 inch [1.6 millimeters] of ice as smooth as Lou Rawls' baritone, as shimmering as hand-blown Bohemian crystal?"

Now that many arenas have two ice resurfacers between periods, the Zamboni hypnotists must mesmerize in half the time.

PEANUTS: ©United Feature Syndicate, Inc.

Model K

Even though by 1963 most Zamboni machines had been redesigned to use an auger to convey the snow into the tank, the unusual Model K retained the paddle system and was built from 1964 to 1969.

Hazards on the Ice

At a top speed of 9 miles (14.5 kilometers) per hour, it doesn't seem like much can go wrong. Just ask any Zamboni driver, however, and you'll hear about close calls at slow speeds. Coins, buttons, and paraphernalia that fans throw on the ice can clog up a Zamboni and delay an event. "Pucks! Any sort of debris will shut down the Zamboni for hours," warns Walt Bruley. "At one college game, someone even threw a shoe on the ice."

At Joe Louis Arena, home of the Detroit Red Wings, fans have been known to throw octopi onto the ice during playoff games for good luck. In most cases, a penalty is called for delay of game. The tradition began in 1952, when Detroit fish merchants Pete and Jerry Cusimano threw an octopus onto the old Olympia Stadium ice (the eight legs, they reasoned, represented the eight victories needed to secure a Stanley Cup in that six-team era). During one game in the 1995 playoffs, fans threw 16 octopi onto the ice. Arena manager and Zamboni driver Al Sobotka ceremoniously scoops them up and game play resumes.

With limited visibility of the area in front of the Zamboni, a driver relies on intuition and good peripheral vision to spot any hazards. During the average hockey game, a Zamboni resurfaces the ice four times (once before the game and once after each period), logging one hour per game. Each year, the average Zamboni is used 800 hours, which is the equivalent of driving 40,000 miles (64,000 kilometers).

Olympia's Zamboni

This Zamboni Model F illustrates an early use of the machines to sell ad space while performing its originally intended duty: smoothing the ice for the Detroit Red Wings at Olympia Stadium. It was in this building in 1952, that fishmongers Pete and Jerry Cusimano began the Detroit tradition of throwing octopus on the ice, creating a potential obstacle for Zamboni drivers. *Walter P. Reuther Library, Wayne State University*

Zamboni Driver of the Year

To celebrate the 50th anniversary of the company in 1999, Zamboni ran a worldwide contest for fans to vote for the "Zamboni Driver of the Year." Ballots were cast via the Internet, and once news of the contest spread, more than 500 e-mails stormed the Zamboni Web site. In the few weeks after the competition was announced, more than 300,000 ballots were cast.

In the final days of the contest, the duel was down to two main competitors: Jimmy "Iceman" MacNeil of Brantford, Ontario, and Al Sobotka, who cleans the ice at Detroit's Joe Louis Arena, home of the NHL Red Wings. The Canadians took the matter to heart and supporting MacNeil became a source of national pride. After all, MacNeil cleared the ice at the Brantford Civic Centre in Wayne Gretzky's hometown.

The sheer number of ballots crashed the Zamboni Web site a few times in the final days, and the California-based company was devoting much more time than it had planned to run a fair contest. Cathy Zamboni, who lives in Brantford, remarked that "Reaction was far more than we expected and [despite] as much fun as we've had, it'll be a relief to have it over. There are other things we need to work on."

The deluge of over one million votes left the Zamboni staff scrambling to make sense of what they thought would be a simple contest. More than 200,000 questionable votes had to be tossed, as the official judges were wary of ballot-box stuffers. Cheers rang across Canada when it was announced that MacNeil had trounced Sobotka, 177,560 votes to 97,265.

After the hard-fought battle, Detroit's Sobotka told Brantford, Ontario's *The Expositor*: "Jimmy got his dream come true. I could tell it had meaning for him." The American Zamboni driver couldn't resist throwing in a little jab, though, stating, "I made this contest. If it wasn't for me, this contest would be nothing."

The contest culminated at the NHL All-Star game in Toronto, where Richard Zamboni awarded MacNeil a Zamboni-shaped trophy.

There are four steps in the process of making perfect ice: shaving, collecting, washing, and renewing. The sharp blade of the Zamboni ice resurfacer shaves off a very thin layer of the top ice. This stainless-steel blade weighs 57 pounds (26 kilograms) and is sharp enough to saw through stacks of newspapers. The resulting snow is whisked away by giant augers, or screw conveyors, that carry it to the center of the machine's rear. From there, the shavings are conveyed up to the snow tank and then dumped at the end of each resurfacing. Water jets inside the conditioner spray the ice, which both flushes out any debris and fills grooves left by skates. A vacuum pump sucks up the extra water and a final layer of warm water (some facilities heat their resurfacing water up to 140 degrees Fahrenheit [60 degrees Celsius]) is sprayed on the ice. A giant towel smoothes the water to leave a glimmering sheet of ice that is frozen by the refrigeration equipment beneath the ice rink.

While it may seem like the machine does all the work, Walt Bruley regards ice resurfacing as an art. "You have to take into consideration air temperature, humidity, ice temperature, how much water. Too much hot water won't freeze, but if the ice is too thin, it can go down to the concrete. [You have to check the] fuel, water,

continued on page 65

Limited Visibility

Zamboni drivers rely on intuition when clearing the ice. On this Model B—legendary No. 4 restored and on display at the U.S. Hockey Hall of Fame—the driver had to look through a small area under the snow tank and above the Willys Jeep body on which it was built. One wave to the kids in the stands could land the machine in the dasher boards.

Side Projects: A Zamboni by Any Other Name . . .

As a Renaissance man of machines, Frank Zamboni didn't limit his creativity to ice resurfacing, but branched out into less well-known vehicles:

Zamboni Vault Carrier. A cemetery near Paramount asked Frank to design a machine to lift and carry around heavy cement burial vaults so the concrete tombs could be moved to the final resting spot.

Zamboni Black Widow. After the concrete burial vault was dropped into the ground, the Black Widow would clean up. "When the ceremony was all over," Richard explains, "the Black Widow would push all the dirt back in the ground over the top [of the vault]."

Astro Zamboni. The Monsanto Chemical Company asked Frank for help with its Astroturf product because water wouldn't drain into the ground like it did with natural grass. So Frank rigged a machine that sucked 400 gallons (1,514 liters) of water per minute. Water is extracted and then sprayed out the side. The Astro Zamboni is credited with preventing a few World Series games from being rained out. Once when Frank was showing off the Astro Zamboni, he accidentally doused a KSD radio and TV announcer with water and then "sent him a bottle of

When the Monsanto Chemical Company asked Frank Zamboni for help because water wouldn't drain through its Astroturf like it did through natural grass, Frank rigged a machine that sucked 400 gallons (1,514 liters) of water per minute.

Chivas Regal or some kind of nice Scotch to apologize," according to Richard.

Frank Zamboni also invented a machine that removed painted lines on Astroturf so various sports could be played on the same field. Rotary brushes scrubbed the turf and then blasted the surface with a high-pressure stream of water. The loosened paint was then sucked up.

Zamboni Grasshopper. To lay down huge rolls of Astroturf in a hurry, Frank Zamboni invented a machine to fill football fields with green. A U.S. patent was granted in 1978 and the Grasshopper was used at indoor stadiums such as the Louisiana Superdome. Richard remembers testing the Grasshopper by turning the streets next to the factory into temporary green lawns.

To lay down huge rolls of Astroturf in a hurry, Frank Zamboni invented the Grasshopper, which was used at indoor stadiums such as the Louisiana Superdome, seen here.

Shaving

A blade ❶ shaves the surface of the ice.

Collecting

After a horizontal screw ❷ gathers the shavings, a vertical screw ❸ propels them into the snow tank ❹.

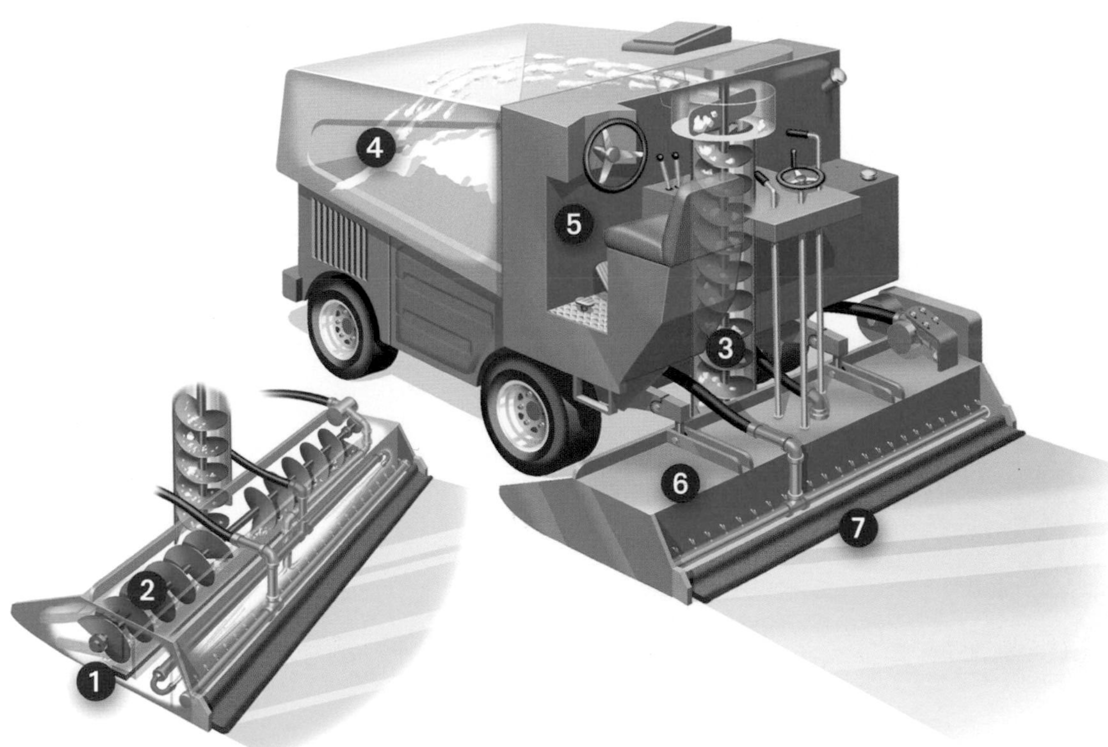

Washing

Water is fed from a wash-water tank ❺ to a squeegee-like "conditioner" ❻, which smooths the ice. Dirty water is vacuumed, filtered, and returned to the tank.

Renewing

Clean hot water is spread on the ice by a towel ❼ behind the conditioner.

How It Works

A look at the inner workings of the Coolest Machine on Ice. *George Retseck*

Shoveling Snow

Before the revolutionary Zamboni Model G—the first to ditch the Willys Jeep—in 1963 allowed the snow to be automatically dumped, Zamboni drivers had to hop into the snow tank at the end of the night and shovel out the ice shavings. This driver is clearing out a vintage Model E.

continued from page 60

tires and make sure the pathway is clear. No debris on ice!" The water must be constantly regulated so that it freezes properly but doesn't turn to slush.

Then there are the fans, perhaps the biggest hazard of all. When the pep band broke into a sultry striptease number at a Clarkson University game, an overeducated and perhaps over-inebriated student slowly disrobed to catcalls from the audience, suggestively throwing his shirt on the ice just as the Zamboni was passing. The shirt was chopped up by the blades and sucked into the machine, and the machine clunked to a stop. The near-naked student risked hypothermia in the frigid arena as he fell prey to jeers from the impatient crowd that wanted the

Snow in Summer

Zamboni drivers rejoiced at the Model G and its automatic snow dumper.

Snow in Summer

What better way to spend a summer afternoon than having a snowball fight outside the local arena, thanks to the dumping tank aboard the Zamboni Model 500?

game to resume. Harvard coach Bill Cleary told *Sports Illustrated*, "Forty-five minutes later, everything is fixed, but we're frozen to death. Clarkson scores three or four goals, and it's all over for us."

Zamboni Snow Cone Machine

In 1964, the Zamboni ice resurfacer was completely redesigned. The Jeep chassis was retired and the chain of paddles that conveyed the snow into the tank was discontinued, replaced by a vertical screw. Most importantly to drivers, a new snow-dumping mechanism was added.

"I used to maintain the ice at the old Curling Club before it burned down in the 1970s," recalls Duluth's "Zamboni Man," Walt Bruley. The hockey arena was on the third floor. "We had to shovel the snow out from the third-floor window. By mid-January, the pile would reach all the way up to the third floor, so we had to go out and shovel off the snowdrift because we couldn't get out. It wasn't until mid-July that it'd all melt."

Today, each time a Zamboni resurfaces a hockey rink, about 60 cubic feet (4.25 cubic meters) of "snow" (approximately 1,500 pounds [680 kilograms]) is shaved and gathered in the machine's snow tank. If the shavings were clean, kids could line up for 3,661 snow cones made of fresh Zamboni ice. With each run, as the shavings are cleared, approximately 140 to 150 gallons (530 to 570 liters) of water are left to freeze on the ice.

Piles of snow gathered outside ice arenas from Zamboni tanks are a familiar site around the world, and in all seasons. "I remember when my dad would dump all the snow out on the streets and we'd have snowball fights in the middle of summer in

continued on page 71

Side Dumper

This little Zamboni JR (for Junior) had a special side hatch for easy access to unload the ice shavings at the end of the evening. For the Model JR, the company even considered using the automatic clutch from Space Age Salsbury scooters, built in nearby Pomona. "We just didn't have enough speed on the Zamboni to shift it up," Richard remembers of clutch experiments. "It works fine on scooters, but not on a Zamboni."

"Underneath the Hood"

In 2003, Zamboni further increased the power and efficiency of the 500 Series with the introduction of the Model 540, which features a 2.5-liter, 4-cylinder overhead-valve liquid-cooled 63-horsepower engine.

International Zamboni

Zamboni Company has dealers and distributors to serve customers worldwide. With a distributor in Zurich, Switzerland, Zamboni makes sure its ice resurfacers are a common sight on rinks across Europe. Here a Rolba Zamboni smoothes the ice at the 1976 Winter Olympics in Innsbruck.

continued from page 67

Southern California," Frank's granddaughter, Mary Ann Russell, reminisces.

Zamboni watchers may question why headlights are mounted on the front of the machine when it invariably clears the ice under the lights of an arena. The headlights serve to shine the path for the Zamboni to dump the snow outside at night or even to travel to a different arena in the wee hours.

Maintain That Zamboni!

Once a Zamboni is in the hands of new drivers, they must keep their beloved ice resurfacer properly tuned. The Zamboni Company can't provide maintenance for all 8,000 ice resurfacers ever made. "The components of the machine are easily repaired by mechanics around the world, with assistance from our factory's customer service department," explains Paula Coony from Zamboni.

Zamboni Junior

This early Zamboni JR has paddles on a conveyor belt to haul ice shavings from the back of the machine to the snow tank. Thanks to the factory in Paramount, this Zamboni ice resurfacer has been fully restored to perfect condition.

Zamboni Factory
Frank Zamboni proudly emblazoned his name on the front of his factory. His inventions were often a bit more mysterious to curious onlookers who wondered what sort of magic went on behind those corrugated walls.

Inside Zamboni
The Zamboni company gets constant requests from hockey and figure-skating buffs to tour the place where the world's most famous ice resurfacers are born. The factory is a working industrial area, though, and not nearly as glamorous as the end result: the Zamboni ice resurfacers.

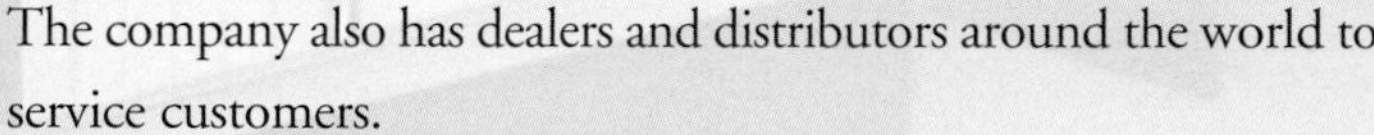

The company also has dealers and distributors around the world to service customers.

With proper care, a Zamboni ice resurfacer will easily last 10 to 15 years and can even last 35 to 40 years. "Part of the problem is also one of Zamboni & Co.'s strengths: Their ice resurfacers last more than 20 years," *USA Today* reported in 1985. Much of Zamboni's business comes from replacing machines at ice rinks, but planned obsolescence is thrown out the window when some machines last 50 years. "They do last a little longer than we would like," Richard Zamboni told the Minneapolis *Star Tribune* in 1990.

While electric Zamboni machines are popular because they don't emit exhaust in enclosed arenas, they cost more and require a broader knowledge of electrical systems to maintain. Gas engines, on the other hand, require good ventilation and proper tuning when used indoors, but are more familiar to mechanics.

The Factory

"This one's going to Austria; this one's going to China," Richard Zamboni says while leading a tour of the small Zamboni factory in Paramount, California. The ice resurfacers are shipped around the world, but for all their fame, they are hand-built one by one, just like Ferrari cars half a world away. In this age of giant mechanized robots building most cars at dizzying speeds, each Zamboni ice resurfacer is constructed, painted, and completed in about three weeks with no assembly lines or robotics. Because each machine is custom-built by the 30 to 35 employees to the exact specifications of the customer, orders for new machines are taken six months out.

To keep up with demand, a second Zamboni factory was opened in Paris, Ontario, in 1967 and then moved to nearby Brantford, the hometown of Wayne Gretzky. Since Canada

continued on page 76

Double Zamboni

As shown here in front of the factory in Paramount, the giant Model G required two operators to smooth the ice: one to steer and the other to shave and squirt. Only one Model G designed for two operators was built, and it was shipped to Japan. Later Model G (four units) machines were built for one operator.

Breaking Down Borders

Zamboni ended the Cold War? In 1961, the Ice Capades went bravely behind the Iron Curtain with its own Zamboni ice resurfacer. Awed by this newfangled capitalist technology, the Soviets managed to hold on to the Zamboni machine after the Ice Capades left Moscow. The Russians were so impressed that numerous Zamboni ice resurfacers were ordered and sent to the U.S.S.R. before the wall came down.

Zamboni machines have also been sold into the Chinese market as that country's recreation industry has grown, while at least 200 machines have been exported to Japan. In 1987 *Sports Illustrated* claimed, "There are Zambonis in a majority of arenas in North America. There are Zambonis behind the Iron Curtain, Zambonis near China's Great Wall, in Australia, Korea, South Africa. Geography doesn't matter; politics matter even less. Ice is ice."

By plane, truck, or boat, Zamboni ice resurfacers travel the world and even infiltrated the Iron Curtain during the Cold War, thanks to the Ice Capades and Winter Olympics.

Zamboni Offices

The 1960s Southern California architecture of the Zamboni headquarters in Paramount fits right into its balmy surroundings, shattering visions of a factory on the tundra.

continued frpm page 72

invented the game of hockey and thousands of rinks fill the country to allow everyone to indulge in the national sport, a Zamboni factory seemed appropriate to keep up with the world's largest market for ice resurfacers.

Frank Zamboni, grandson of the Zamboni inventor, moved to Canada in 1983 to take up the helm at the Canadian plant. He told *The Expositor* in Brantford, Ontario, in 1999, "I didn't have to join the business. In fact, Dad encouraged me to get out and do different things, which I did until I was 27 when I moved to

Model C

The Zamboni trial track is the Iceland Skating Rink, just a few blocks from the factory in Paramount. A forced-air pipe organ still plays music for figure skaters in search of a chilly reprieve from the hot Southern California sun.

Iceland
PARAMOUNT CALIF.

Dumper

The Model F was eventually updated to have hydraulic lifts. On later models, the dumper was "streamlined" into the body of the machine for the familiar refrigerator-box look.

Air-Conditioning is Extra

This sporty Model 540 features an enclosed cab to protect drivers from inclement weather on outdoor rinks.

Canada. I go back to California monthly for business meetings, but I feel I'm Canadian."

The Zamboni company doesn't give tours because its facilities are busy working factories, but a rare guided tour of the California plant from Richard reveals how a Zamboni machine is born. He points out that, "Rust has always been a problem" so they use a protective undercoating and also "use stainless nuts and bolts and offer galvanized parts." A fiberglass top is used because it's light and doesn't rust. The rear-conditioning unit is usually powder-coated but is also available with galvanized metal.

Zamboni machines are available in electric- or fuel-powered, either by gasoline, propane, or compressed natural gas. Richard notes, "We learned about the electrics from forklift machines. Electrics are one-third more expensive, but cost just pennies a day to run, so they save money in the long run and have no exhaust." For Zamboni spotters, he noted that electric machines have disc brakes on the front and drums on the rear.

Manufacture of some of the Zamboni parts has been shopped out to keep expenses down and quality up. "We don't have a machine shop anymore, but we do have a tire studder,"

continued on page 85

Zamboni Battles the Competition

When Zamboni was declared official ice resurfacer of the National Hockey League in 2002, hockey fans were left scratching their collective heads. "Who else would it be?"

Becky Fisher, a player on the women's hockey team at Cornell University in Ithaca, New York, was stumped. "You mean there's another brand?" She was unaware that her own ice rink was resurfaced by the competition, Olympia, because her team—and most of the world—always referred to all ice resurfacers as "Zambonis."

Over the years, five other manufacturers have tried to get in on the ice-resurfacing business in the United States, but all have given up. Eight Canadian companies have also built ice resurfacers, but only one is still making machines.

The NHL began using Zamboni's machines in 1954, five years after the 1949 debut. Making Zamboni machines its official ice resurfacers in 2002 meant that the NHL could license the Zamboni trademark, shape, and name with its other merchandise. While many fans just had to get their hands on a mini Zamboni with their favorite team's logo emblazoned across the metal body, some were surprised that five NHL teams didn't use Zamboni-brand resurfacers to clear the ice.

The St. Louis Blues put up a Zamboni kiosk to sell shirts in their arena, despite the fact that the competition was cleaning their rink. More understandably, the Vancouver Canucks face off at GM Place, so the ice there is shaved by Olympia machines, whose chassis is made by General Motors. The Carolina Hurricanes convinced stock car legend Richard Petty to film an advertisement for the team atop a zooming Zamboni, but the Hurricanes had to switch filming to a neighboring rink when they realized they had the wrong machine on their home ice.

Richard Zamboni put it succinctly to *Sports Illustrated* in 1987: "I once heard a man say that his company made a better zamboni than Zamboni. I said, 'Sir, only Zamboni can make a Zamboni.'"

INDISPENSABLE FOR

Each Zamboni Ice Resurfacer is the result of over twenty years of research in the field of ice rink resurfacing. An ice rink represents a large investment to its owners, whether the rink be public or private, indoor or outdoor. The speed and economy in reproducing a perfect surface after a session are big factors in getting the maximum use out of this investment and the Zamboni

Ice Resurfa
problem.
The Za
picks up a
squeegees
removes ex
done all at
ing conditi

ECONOMICAL • MORE ICE TIME • EASY

Japanese Zamboni

In front of a crowd of thousands in Karuizawa, Japan, the Zamboni Model G cleared the ice for eager skaters in 1963.

Model 700

The biggest Zamboni model of them all, the 700 is made to resurface giant speed-skating rinks to perfect smoothness. This Model 700 resurfaced at the 1988 Winter Olympics in Calgary, Alberta.

15714
ZAMBONI
ZAMBONI
#8,000
University of Minnesota
Mariucci Arena

continued from page 79

Richard explains. "Studded tires are the last thing [installed] so we don't dull the studs or ruin the floor of the factory." As the *Washington Post* waxed about the clicking of the studs: "It trundles onto the rink like the jolliest possible combination of a circus calliope, a steam iron and a McCormick reaper. One hears the musical crackle of studded tires."

Since the birth of the Model A in 1949, only 8,000 Zamboni ice resurfacers have been hand-built at the Paramount and Brantford factories. Richard proudly shows a photo of the celebration the employees had for No. 8,000—a landmark Zamboni ice resurfacer that went to the University of Minnesota Golden Gophers.

The 8,000th Zamboni represents a radical update from the original Model A. Today's machines use modern engines, hydraulics, and electronic controls. Zamboni ice resurfacers are four-wheel drive and include studded tires for traction around those breakneck curves. In spite of years of updates, Zamboni has never seen the need to adorn the dashboard with an odometer or speedometer—only an hour meter.

And the sticker price? A gas-burning Zamboni 500 Series machine is in the neighborhood of a new Lexus, but the ice-resurfacing benefits offered make it the vehicle of choice. Rival companies may sell their machines at a lower price, but Richard assures visitors that while their competitors may build a good product, "We just feel that we build a better machine." It would seem most customers agree. Zamboni still sells more machines than all their competitors combined.

No. 8,000

Considering the relatively small number of Zamboni ice resurfacers in existence (especially compared to giant automakers), their popularity is enormous. In 2005, the Zamboni factory in Paramount proudly rolled its 8,000th Zamboni ice resurfacer off the line and sent it to the University of Minnesota's Golden Gophers to resurface Mariucci Arena in Minneapolis, Minnesota.

torino 2006
torino

Third Period

Zamboni Zealots

What is it about Zamboni ice resurfacers that inspire such creativity? At least two defunct Zamboni machines have been turned into a barbecue smoker and a giant hot tub. Trick-or-treaters have even been known to dress up as Zambonis for Halloween. A Zamboni ice resurfacer painted like a garbage truck in Duluth, Minnesota, was rigged with special hoses to water the flowers outside around the arena. Of course, the local TV news couldn't resist broadcasting footage that evening.

Martin Zellar of the Gear Daddies—a band that hailed from hockey-mad Minnesota—and the hockey-centric band The Zambonis both penned odes to Zamboni. The Zambonis perform the song "The Great Zamboni of Devotion." French avant-garde musician Jean-François LaPorte even used an ice resurfacer as the main instrument in his "found-sound" composition of

Bringing It All Back Home

Frank Zamboni's mother was born just 19 miles (31 kilometers) from where the 2006 Winter Olympics were held in Torino, Italy. Fittingly, 16 Zamboni machines cleared the ice surfaces used at the Winter Games. ***David Klutho***

Duluth's Zamboni Man

Walt Bruley drives the electric garbage truck–painted Zamboni at the Duluth Entertainment Convention Center arena next to Lake Superior. "I don't want to say I'm famous," Bruley says, "but whenever I go out to dinner in Duluth someone comes up and says, 'You're the guy who drives the Zamboni, right?'"

Zambonis: The Band

Billing themselves as "North America's Favorite ALL-HOCKEY Band," Connecticut-based The Zambonis not only named themselves after the coolest machines on ice, they penned a song entitled "The Great Zamboni of Devotion." ***Courtesy The Zambonis***

Goldy Gopher

The team mascot's biggest rival for the love of their fans is the Zamboni ice resurfacer. The University of Minnesota's Goldy Gopher poses next to the advertisement-laden machine in Mariucci Arena before a spin-and-grin tour around the ice.

Another Milestone

The Zamboni staff poses with No. 8,000 outside the Paramount factory.

musique concrète that lasts more than 22 minutes (longer than it takes to resurface a rink).

Nicknames, typically true signs of affection, abound for the boxy ice resurfacer, which at various times has been referred to as the "Dean Machine of Rinksmanship," a "Member of the Clean Plate Club," and the wordy "America's Best-Loved Self-Propelled Athletic Surface Maintenance Device."

Writers have likewise mused on the mesmerizing Zamboni ice resurfacer. The *Washington Post* described its movement as "ungainliness reminiscent of *Fantasia*'s ballet of hippos in tutus," and *Sports Illustrated* declared, "It looked as though it had been built in a fraternity basement as part of some college-humor contest." And who's to say that the Bard of Avon, William Shakespeare, wasn't jealously envisioning the prowess of future Zamboni machines when he wrote in *King John*, "to smooth the ice, or add another hue unto the rainbow . . . is wasteful and ridiculous excess." What envy!

On the other hand, perhaps some admirers go a bit too far. A man nicknamed "Buggy" begged the driver at the old Curling Club in Duluth, Minnesota, to let him drive the much-loved machine. Buggy worked for almost nothing and would go to the arena late at night just to be with his ice-resurfacing machine. The club's regular driver recalls, "I caught Buggy once kneeling down

continued on page 94

Gear Daddies Drive the Zamboni

Martin Zellar played youth hockey at Riverside Arena in Austin, Minnesota, but spent most of his time watching Smokey the Zamboni driver clear the ice. Like many young skaters, Zellar daydreamed of smoothing the ice like a pro in front of thousands.

Zellar eventually moved north to the Twin Cities with his buddies and formed the band the Gear Daddies. On the heels of Minneapolis punk bands like Hüsker Dü and the Replacements, Zellar's band soared to popularity with upbeat songs and lyrics that could actually be heard over the electric guitars. In spite of a trace of country-western in their sound, the Gear Daddies kept the irreverent punk mentality.

Their brave musical path to do the unexpected led Zellar to convince his record label, Polygram, to include a "hidden track" on the 1990 Gear Daddies LP, *Billy's Live Bait*. In a playful moment, Zellar dashed off a song about his youthful days at Riverside Arena. The one song not listed on the record proved to be its biggest hit. "I Wanna Drive the Zamboni" further cemented Zamboni's image in the public consciousness.

The song became an important part of the soundtrack to the Walt Disney Film *The Mighty Ducks*. Today, it's played at almost every pro hockey game.

"All things being relative, in the old days, (the song) was generating money that seemed like a lot back then," Zellar says of the song, "but I don't get paid when it's played in arenas. That's the big myth. I certainly should. I'll bet Gary Glitter does for his song," Martin says, referring to the ubiquitous "Rock and Roll Part Two" (The Hey Song). "I'll bet he has direct deposit."

In spite of all his other songwriting, Zellar is known in hockey arenas across the United States and Canada for this hit about driving the Zamboni. "Definitely at first, that was a sore spot," he admits. "It certainly isn't even close to sum up my whole body of work. It was an afterthought; I wrote it on a whim. I couldn't have spent more than five minutes writing it—maybe 10 minutes—with just three chords. If you write a love song, you're in competition with a million others. I was lucky enough to find a niche, Zamboni, and thank god."

"It's a somewhat dubious legacy," Zellar concludes, "but in my obituary, I'm sure it'll say that the two things about me are that I'm from Austin, Minnesota, the home of Spam, and that I wrote the Zamboni song."

"I Wanna Drive the Zamboni"

by Martin Zellar & the Gear Daddies

Well, I went down to the local arena
Asked to see the manager man,
He came from his office, said, "Son, can I help you?"
I looked at him and said, "Yes, you can."
I wanna drive the Zamboni . . . hey
I wanna drive the Zamboni . . . Yes I do!

Now ever since I was young, it's been my dream
That I might drive a Zamboni machine.
I'd get that ice just as slick as could be,
And all the kids would look up to me.
I wanna drive the Zamboni . . . hey
I wanna drive the Zamboni . . . Yes I do!

Now the manager said, "Son, I know it looks keen,
But that right there is one expensive machine.
And I've got Smokey who's been driving for years."
About that time, I broke down in tears.
'Cause I wanna drive the Zamboni . . . hey
I wanna drive the Zamboni . . . Yes I do!

Rest in Peace

The rumble of the ice resurfacer's engine provides the requiem for this slow-motion funeral procession. Do not go gently into that good night! No, play hockey to commemorate the loyal Zamboni driver who now lies underground at the close of day. *Courtesy John Stennes,* **Grand Forks Herald**

continued from page 91

in front of the Zamboni—he had a special relationship with the Zamboni. He kind of made you nervous." The Zamboni worshipper of Duluth was separated from his beloved when "he drove the Zamboni through the sideboards and we had to fire him."

In fact, almost everyone seems to have a crush on Zamboni machines except for goaltenders. After the Zamboni exits, goalies without fail scrape up the ice in front of the nets to make it less smooth. One reason is so they don't accidentally slip, another is because rough ice slows the puck. Gump Worsley began his storied NHL career with the New York Rangers in 1952 when Zamboni ice resurfacers were just starting to be used. "We'd go around after the game and sneak a peek at it," he later recalled. "It did make the ice smoother so guys could stickhandle better—I didn't like that much."

Zamboni Parades

Small towns that scrimp and save their proceeds from bake sales and cake walks for their very own Zamboni have inevitably run the blocky machines in the annual parade down Main Street. Recently, more high-profile processions have included Zamboni ice resurfacers, which needn't slow down to travel at parade speed.

Minimal Advertising

After a treacherous road trip from Southern California to the hills of the Bay Area, this Zamboni ice resurfacer found a happy home. Compare the small advertising typeface on the side of the snow tank with outrageous modern designs.

Minnesota was devastated when its NHL North Stars left town for—of all places—Dallas, Texas. This slap in the face was forgiven when St. Paul was awarded another NHL team, the Minnesota Wild. More than a dozen Zamboni machines drove through downtown in celebration, and then-Mayor and current U.S. Senator Norm Coleman viewed it as the perfect photo op for the next election.

In 1995, The *Peanuts* characters came alive on a Rotary International float for the Tournament of Roses Parade. Snoopy, the only canine to ever drive an ice resurfacer, proudly drove a Zamboni to cheers from the crowd.

Perhaps the most notable Zamboni parade, however, occurred when the NHL All-Star Game was held in Los Angeles in 2002, just up the road from the Zamboni factory in Paramount. The first

MIDTERM REVIEW
MARCH 5TH
THURSDAY 10:00 ~ 3:00
ART CENTER COLLEGE OF DESIGN
ROOM #222
ALL ARE WELCOME
R.S.V.P. 626.396.2344
RICHARD & DON ZAMBONI
MORE FUN! REMOTE CONTROL BY AUDIENCE! PARTICIPATE!
SNAP ON PARTS EASY TO CHANGE
DISTANCE FROM THE ICE
MIST!
USE STEAM TO SOFTEN THE ICE BEFORE SHAVING WONT DO AS MUCH DAMAGE TO THE BLADE ∴ SOFTER ICE.
HOOVER VACUUM ZAMBONI!
STEERING
KINGS
CLEAR PLASTIC SHELL MORE FUN TO WATCH
TURNING CHAIR

High Design

As an art project to design a souped-up Zamboni ice resurfacer, the NHL's Los Angeles Kings, Zamboni, and the Pasadena Art Center College of Design brainstormed a 25th century Zamboni machine (left). At the end of the day, Richard Zamboni had to spoil some of the hot rod designers' dreams by pointing out that there was no room to store the ice shavings or hot water. *Courtesy Art Center College of Design*

Zamboni ever made, the Model A, which usually rests at Iceland Skating Rink, guided the procession during which one of the vintage machines carried the Stanley Cup. Zamboni Models E, JR, and K followed in the smoke of the A as the ice machines made their way through the balmy streets from City Hall to Staples Center.

Souped-Up Zambonis

Nobody dreamed of covering early Zamboni machines with wild paint schemes. And not until the 1960s did anyone think to use the slow-moving surface of a Zamboni as a canvas for advertising. Seyfert's Potato Chips has the dubious honor of being the first to emblazon their logo across an ice resurfacer, and today most Zamboni machines are covered with ads for everything from burritos to Bud. Advertising on a Zamboni can easily cost $25,000 per year at major arenas.

"School colors are always very popular," Richard Zamboni says. When asked his opinion about some of the wild advertising paint schemes, Richard replies diplomatically, "I have a hard time with some of the colors." Still, Richard is willing to dream about what a Zamboni could look like in the future—along with the students at nearby Pasadena Art Center College of Design.

"The L.A. Kings approached the students and asked them to design something that wasn't this chunky old block of stuff just going around the ice rink," Richard explains. Suddenly, Space Age Zambonis with streamlined designs leaped from the drawing tables. Richard Zamboni loved the new blueprints but had to burst the students' bubble because their designs didn't allow enough space for snow and hot water. "They don't worry about the engineering, just the design," Richard says. With a Zamboni, it's difficult to improve on perfection.

Happy Holidays from Zamboni!

Spreading yuletide cheer to its clients and friends, the Zamboni company pops another artistic vision of its ice resurfacers in the mailbox. *Steve Contreras Design*

Built for Speed

Some drivers—in this case, stock car legend Richard Petty—can't resist putting on a show for the crowd. The average Zamboni machine resurfaces ice 9.7 times per day and spends 116 minutes on the ice, assuming 12 minutes to clean the ice each time. At pokey speeds topping out at 9 miles per hour (14.5 kilometers per hour)—but usually much slower—a Zamboni ice resurfacer typically travels only about 7.3 miles (11.7 kilometers) a day. *Courtesy Carolina Hurricanes*

Something about the Zamboni machines moves drivers to want to imagine them as slick speedsters. In 2005, a *Road & Track* road test of the top-of-the-line Zamboni ice resurfacer reported an acceleration of 0 to 9 miles [14.5 kilometers] per hour in 6.22 seconds.

Truck Trend took their own road test of the Zamboni 500 a little more seriously: "Firewall the throttle (at 3500 rpm), mash the pedal, and you'll travel 60 ft [18m] in 6.22 seconds at 8.25 mph [13.28km/h], the studded tires scrambling for grip. Braking is even easier—just release the pedal and the rear drums bring the ice resurfacer from a full-throttle 9 mph [14.5km/h] to a halt in 31 ft [9m]." The *Truck Trend* test also put the Zamboni 500 through a slalom course at 4.5 miles (7.2 kilometers) per hour—a quick walking pace.

The real test track for Zamboni machines, however, is at Iceland Skating Rink, a few blocks from the California factory. To get to the arena, the machines are driven through the roads of Paramount. Local cops turn a blind eye to the machines' lack of

continued on page 103

Gold Zamboni

The now-classic blue and white paint scheme wasn't established by the time this Model HDA was ready. The bright metallic paint jobs of the Willys Jeep days aren't available today. "We can't do metallics anymore and they're so hard to touch up," Richard Zamboni explains.

Zamboni
FRANK J. ZAMBONI & CO.
PARAMOUNT, CALIF.
PAT. & PATS. PEND.
ICE RE-SURFACER

ZAMBONI

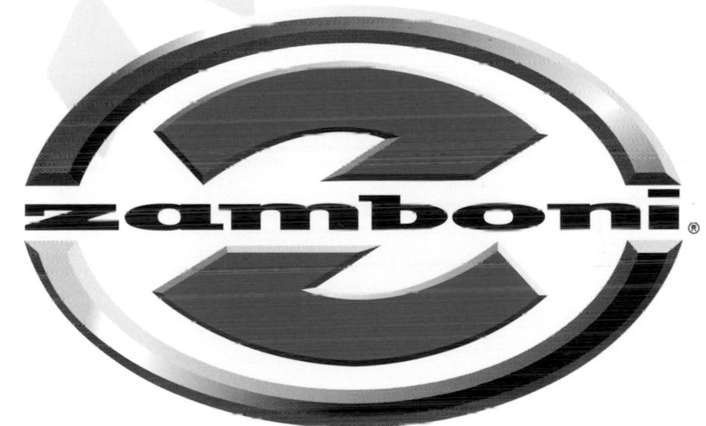

Evolution of a Logo

While the most recognized emblem of the ice resurfacers is the blocky ZAMBONI lettering emblazoned on the front of the machines, the company has fiddled with different designs over the years.

ARENA
AISLE
WILLYS

continued from 98

license plates, turn signals, or anything else that would make them street legal. Impatient motorists zoom past the slow-motion machines that inspired a journalist from the *Washington Post* to exaggerate the ice resurfacers' prowess: "Though four-wheeled, the Zamboni circles the rink with the deft tracking motion one associates with three-wheeled vehicles, like F-16s moving up to the flight line."

Richard Zamboni is sometimes seen out on the streets of Paramount test driving a new machine. "Just the other day, I was driving the [Zamboni] Junior back from Iceland. As I'm driving on the city streets, I saw a police car." Richard hunched his shoulders as though he was nervous that he'd be thrown in the clink for his Zamboni road trip. "The sheriff rolls down his window and waves at me. I just hope I wasn't doing anything wrong!"

Zamboni Road Trips

Taking a Zamboni on a joy ride is many a kid's dream. Stories abound of hijacked Zambonis from local ice arenas taken for late-night road trips to the drive-thru at the Jack In The Box. "Oh, there's always stories about kids breaking in and going on a joy ride," Paula Coony of Zamboni acknowledges.

One of the most impressive Zamboni road trips was also one of the earliest. In 1950, when Norwegian skating sensation Sonja Henie simply had to have a Zamboni of her own, Frank Zamboni agreed to deliver the machine to her skating troupe. The earliest Zamboni machines were built around a Willys Jeep decked out with ice-resurfacing machinery. Frank loaded up all the accessories

continued on page 106

Sonja's Zamboni

When Norwegian skating superstar Sonja Henie performed at Frank Zamboni's Iceland Skating Rink in Paramount, California, she witnessed the bizarre contraption that Frank had rigged up to clear the ice. Immediately, she knew she needed one of her own to bring on the road. Frank updated his Model A and sold Sonja Zamboni Nos. 2 and 3 to tour the country.

Zamboni Wipeout!

Even though Zamboni resurfacers drive slowly and steadily on the ice, somehow they occasionally manage to get themselves into terrible predicaments. One of the most frequent traps is the curved corner of hockey rinks. At the DECC in Duluth, Minnesota, the Zamboni man recalls, "Once I got the bumper stuck and then the rear got stuck too. It took two [hockey] teams and two bottle jacks to get it out."

One of the earliest Zamboni wipeouts was executed by Frank Zamboni himself, not on an ice rink but out on California State Highway 99. Frank was delivering a Zamboni Model C—

When a pin fell out of the steering column on the way to Berkeley, Frank Zamboni was left with an out-of-control ice resurfacer on California Highway 99. Luckily, the Model C went off the road gently and avoided telephone poles and oncoming traffic.

No. 5—450 miles (724 kilometers) from the factory north to the Berkeley Iceland rink in the 1950s. His cousin Henry Masoero followed closely in a car and signaled for traffic to pass the slow-moving convoy. When a cotter pin popped out of the steering column of the Zamboni machine, Frank was left helplessly spinning the steering wheel. The out-of-control Model C crashed into oleander bushes on the side of the road. Fortunately, Frank was driving at pokey Zamboni speeds and was just a bit shaken. He and his cousin towed No. 5 out of the ditch, replaced the cotter pin, and delivered the machine to its new home.

Years later, a Zamboni was driven out on a frozen lake in Keystone, Colorado, to smooth a rink. In the middle of winter, this maneuver shouldn't be any problem since cars regularly zoom across frozen lakes. The 3-ton machine, however, cracked the ice and plunged into the frigid water. "After it fell through the ice, they had to go through the whole machine to get it working again," Richard Zamboni remembers.

Frank drove Zamboni No. 10 from the Paramount factory in Southern California to Sutro's in the San Francisco Bay Area. The only way to deliver the machine onto the ice below, however, was down this steep temporary ramp from the upper level. With hardly any brakes, the Zamboni ice resurfacer with Frank aboard was slowly lowered with a rope. If the rope hadn't held the 3-ton machine, Frank would have sped down the ramp, across the ice, out the giant glass windows, and down a cliff into the Pacific Ocean. Following this harrowing experience, Frank thought twice about personally delivering his ice resurfacers.

Underwater Zamboni
Three tons of Zamboni need thick ice to keep the steering wheel above water. This Zamboni ice resurfacer took a plunge in Keystone, Colorado. Frogmen and cranes were called in to save the Zamboni submarine from the deep.

continued from page 103

into a trailer attached to the Jeep and drove across country in the middle of winter to meet Sonja in St. Louis. Frank nearly froze driving the Zamboni machine across the Great Plains. When he finally arrived in St. Louis, Sonja's show had already moved on to Chicago. In spite of being half-frozen, Frank hung a left and delivered the Zamboni to Chicago Stadium.

Frank's son Richard Zamboni recalls the end of the trip in Chicago, where he and his father had dinner with Sonja and the second of her three husbands, Winthrop Gardner. At the Cameo Restaurant, Richard admired the restaurant's large wooden pepper mill. "Sonja told me, 'If you like it, just take it,'" Richard recalls. While hesitant, he did and still has the pepper mill to this day. Richard remembers his father later telling him, "I think Sonja owns the place."

Not until 2002 was Frank Zamboni's road trip surpassed. In preparation for the 2002 Winter Olympics in Salt Lake City, Utah, Jimmy MacNeil of Brantford, Ontario, checked the oil on his Zamboni and set out on the longest voyage on an ice-resurfacing machine in history. He left the east coast of Canada at St. John's, Newfoundland, in the fall of 2001 and began his cross-country trip during the coldest months of winter at 9 miles (14.5 kilometers) per hour.

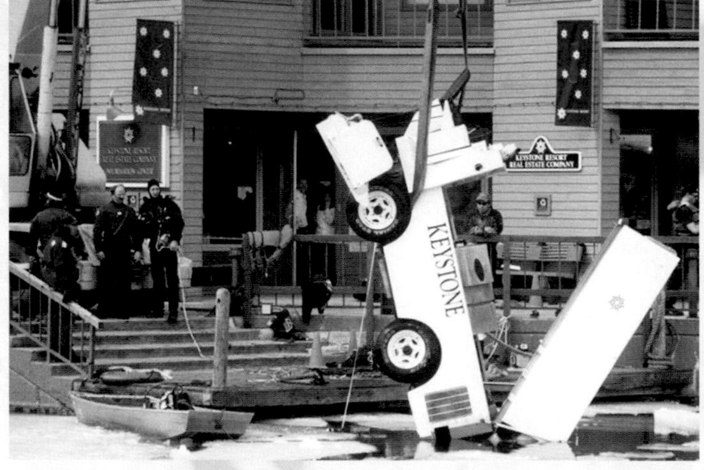

As the Brantford Civic Centre's Zamboni man and his slow-motion convoy putzed into each town along the way, Canadians offered an instant parade down main street.

Twice the Fun

The since-demolished Met Center in Bloomington, Minnesota, was the first NHL rink to clear its ice with dueling ice resurfacers, now common practice. This photo was taken at "the Met" on December 6, 1990. As for the machines themselves, the newspaper caption said it all: "The marvelous, mellifluous name is just part of the Zamboni's appeal. The strange-looking machine that cleans slushy surfaces in ice rinks across the continent is a favorite among kids of all ages."
Brian Peterson, Courtesy **Minneapolis Star Tribune**

MacNeil's four-month voyage took him across the prairies and over the Rocky Mountains to Vancouver, British Columbia. After he reached the Canadian west coast, MacNeil's "Drive for Gold" was forever emblazoned in the hallowed annals of the Zamboni hall of fame.

Dueling Zamboni Machines

Resurfacing ice typically takes less than 15 minutes, depending on the skill of the Zamboni driver, who follows one of three basic patterns: the common double outside loop, the uncommon crosscut, or a figure eight. In the late 1980s, two Minnesota

continued on page 113

ZAMBONI ICE RESURFACER

indispensable for efficient ice rink management

New Model HD

shaves the ice • picks up the snow • washes and squeegies applies water for new ice IN ONE OPERATION

results in SUPERB ICE CARE ★ SURFACE AS SMOOTH AS A MIRROR ★ IMPECCABLE CHAMPIONSHIP RINKS ★ SHORT RESURFACING TIME (abt. 20,000 sq. ft. in 10-12 min.) ★ MORE ICE TIME FOR SKATERS

See it in action at Silver Blades Ice Rinks :— Streatham London, Birmingham, Sheffield, Bradford, Bristol. Queens Ice Skating Club, Bayswater, London. Sportsdrome Ltd., Richmond Ice Rink, East Twickenham. Crossmyloof Ice Rink, Glasgow.

ROLBA LTD. Charlwoods Rd., East Grinstead, East Sussex
Tel. No.: East Grinstead 22278/9

....A Perfect Skating Surface with the

ZAMBONI Ice Resurfacer....

INDISPENSABLE FOR EFFICIENT ICE RINK OPERATION

Each Zamboni Ice Resurfacer is the result of over twenty years of research in the field of ice rink resurfacing. An ice rink represents a large investment to its owners, whether the rink be public or private, indoor or outdoor. The speed and economy in reproducing a perfect surface after a session are big factors in getting the maximum use out of this investment and the Zamboni Ice Resurfacer is the modern answer to this problem.

The Zamboni Ice Resurfacer shaves the ice, picks up and collects all the snow, washes and squeegees behind the blade, applies fresh water, removes excessive water. These operations can be done all at once or singly depending on the changing conditions of your ice.

FAST, ECONOMICAL • MORE ICE TIME • EASY TO OPERATE • MORE PROFIT

MODEL HD (Illustrated above)
Features a time saving snow dump tank for quick unloading.

MODEL K
An improved Non-Dumping standard size ice resurfacer replacing the Model F.

ZAMBONI JR.
A small, manuverable machine designed for rinks of approximately 5000 sq. feet.

Patents:
United States Pat. No. 2,642,679
2,763,939
3,044,193
Canadian Pat. No. 519619
Great Britain Pat. No. 722880
Swiss Pat. No. 319606
W. German Pat. No. 1096261
Other U.S. and Foreign Patents applied for.

FRANK J. ZAMBONI & CO.
8041 EAST JACKSON STREET — PARAMOUNT, CALIFORNIA — MEtcalf 3-1171 CABLE FJZICE

THE *Zamboni*

ICE RE-SURFACING MACHINE

- MUCH SMOOTHER SURFACE
- MORE ICE TIME
- REDUCES WATER BILLS
- REDUCES POWER BILLS
- REDUCES GENERAL EXPENSE

Patents Applied for in the United States and Foreign Countries.

Brilliant Performer! Amazingly Thrifty!

THE RESULT OF YEARS OF RESEARCH AND TESTING THE ZAMBONI ICE RESURFACING MACHINE GIVES A SUPERIOR SURFACE IN A FRACTION OF THE TIME USED BY OLD METHODS.

WHAT THE RINK OPERATORS SAY —

I would like to express our great and complete satisfaction with the Zamboni Ice Re-Surfacing Machine. Our ice now is truly as "smooth as a sheet of glass", a condition we were never able to achieve under the old method of re-surfacing.
Phil Henderson, Jr., Mgr.
PASADENA WINTER GARDEN, Inc.

Words will not express our enthusiasm for the new Zamboni ice re-surfaeer. Under no circumstances would we want to be without your machine and go back to the old method.
Robert A. Bratton, Mgr.
Whitneys-SUTROS
San Francisco, California

The time required to re-surface our ice (20,000 sq. ft.) has been reduced from 45 minutes to 13 minutes by use of the Zamboni Ice Re-Surfacing Machine. And the quality of the surface is much improved. I highly recommend that every rink should have one.
Louis C. Owen, Mgr.
EAST BAY ICELAND
Berkeley, Calif.

SEE THIS REVOLUTIONARY TIME SAVER IN OPERATION AT RINKS AND SHOWS AT THE CHICAGO ARENA; PASADENA WINTER GARDEN; ICELAND, BERKELEY, CALIF.; SUTRO'S, SAN FRANCISCO; DENVER UNIVERSITY RINK; PHILADELPHIA SKATING CLUB; ICELAND, PARAMOUNT, CALIF. — AT ICE CAPADES, ICE FOLLIES, SONJA HENIE ICE REVUE, HOLIDAY ON ICE SHOWS.

Inquiries are invited.
FRANK J. ZAMBONI & CO., PARAMOUNT, CALIFORNIA

PATENTS:
United States NOs. 2,642,679
2,763,939
Canada PAT. NO. 519619
Great Britain NO. 722880
Other U.S. & Foreign Patents Applied for.

FROM EVERY ANGLE
Zamboni
ICE RE-SURFACER
SAVES TIME AND MONEY

See This Revolutionary Time Saver in Operation at Rinks and Shows:

ICE CAPADES
WHITNEYS-SUTROS
BOSTON ARENA
CLEVELAND S. C.
MONTREAL FORUM
PHILADELPHIA S. C.
McGILL UNIVERSITY
TOWER CABANA CLUB
CASINO ICE PALACE
R.P.I. FIELD HOUSE
ST. PAUL AUDITORIUM
S. C. OF BOSTON
MICHIGAN STATE U.
CITY OF JERSEY CITY
CITY OF PHILADELPHIA
NORTHFIELD PLAZA RINK
PHOENIX ICE RINK
ROCHESTER TECH.
BERKELEY ICELAND
KIRBY'S ICE BOWL
BOSTON GARDEN
DALLAS ICE ARENA
PHILADELPHIA ARENA
BOWDOIN COLLEGE
PARAMOUNT ICELAND
HOLIDAY ON ICE
DENVER U. ICE RINK
R. I. AUDITORIUM
LYNN SPORTS CENTER
DETROIT F.S. CLUB
LAVAL SPORTS CENTRE
OLD YORK ROAD CORP.
PASADENA WINTER GARDEN
ALBUQUERQUE ICE ARENA
WILLOW BROOK SPORTS CENTER
CITY OF LONG BEACH, N. Y.
PACIFIC NATIONAL EXHIBITION
WILMETTE RECREATION BOARD
WISSAHICKON SKATING CLUB

THIS BRILLIANT PERFORMER SOLVES ICE MAKING PROBLEMS FOR GOOD...

THIS WORLD FAMOUS INVENTION RE-SURFACES THE ICE WITH A MIRROR-LIKE FINISH IN A FRACTION OF THE TIME USED BY PREVIOUS METHODS.

Easy and economical to operate, the Zamboni Ice Re-surfacer shaves the ice, squeegies it, brushes and washes it, all in one uniquely engineered operation. It maintains a uniform thickness of ice and produces an unrivalled skating floor with a surface as smooth as glass.

CHECK these outstanding ZAMBONI ICE RE-SURFACER FEATURES:

- SAVES TIME.
- BETTER ICE.
- ECONOMY OF OPERATION.
- MORE ICE TIME.
- CUTS WATER BILLS.
- CUTS MANPOWER COSTS
- SIMPLE TO OPERATE.
- LOWER POWER COSTS.
- CUTS GENERAL EXPENSE.

*The NEW, improved 1957 ZAMBONI Ice Re-surfacer is just seven feet in height, much more compact. It will now carry 103 cubic feet of snow (1½ more than previous models). It can also be made to carry 140 cubic feet of snow to take care of large, ... It carries approximately 190 gallons of water to make ice. It also has an improved Vickers Hydraulic System to operate the ... veyor. The cantilever hood folds back easily for routine engine inspection and maintenance.

Inquiries are invited:
FRANK J. ZAMBONI & CO.,
PARAMOUNT, CALIFORNIA

The *Zamboni* for **ICE RE-SURFACER**

- BETTER ICE
- SAVES TIME
- ECONOMICAL
- MORE ICE TIME
- CUTS WATER BILLS
- SIMPLE TO OPERATE
- CUTS POWER COSTS
- CUTS GENERAL EXPENSE

this... ***BRILLIANT PERFORMER SAVES TIME AND MONEY***

THIS WORLD FAMOUS INVENTION RE-SURFACES THE ICE WITH A MIRROR-LIKE FINISH IN A FRACTION OF THE TIME USED BY PREVIOUS METHODS.

Easy and economical to operate, the Zamboni Ice Re-surfacer shaves the ice, squeegies it, brushes and washes it, all in one uniquely engineered operation. It maintains a uniform thickness of ice and produces an unrivalled skating floor with a surface as smooth as glass.

See This Revolutionary Time Saver in Operation at Rinks and Shows:

ICE CAPADES
HOLIDAY ON ICE SHOWS
SONJA HENIE ICE REVUE
PASADENA WINTER GARDEN
BERKELEY ICELAND
WHITNEYS-SUTROS
DENVER U. ICE RINK
PHILADELPHIA S. C.
PARAMOUNT ICELAND
KIRBY'S ICE BOWL
CASINO ICE PALACE
PHILADELPHIA ARENA
PITTSBURGH GARDEN
R. I. AUDITORIUM
BOSTON ARENA
BOSTON GARDEN
LYNN SPORTS CENTRE
CLEVELAND S. C.
HERSHEY SPORTS ARENA
LAVAL SPORTS CENTER
ALBUQUERQUE ICE ARENA
DALLAS ICE ARENA
R. P. I. FIELD HOUSE

Inquiries are invited:
FRANK J. ZAMBONI & CO.,
PARAMOUNT, CALIFORNIA

Proud of the Cup

This Model F reminds Toronto fans of one of the Maple Leafs' three consecutive Stanley Cups (1962 to 1964) as the click-click of the paddles scoops up the snow into the tank.

No. 21: From Boston to Toronto

In 1954, the Boston Bruins became the first NHL team to acquire a Zamboni ice resurfacer. The machine not only cleared the ice at Boston Garden, it was also used to promote the Boston Celtics and Harlem Globetrotters basketball teams. Later, the Model E (No. 21) was completely refurbished by the Zamboni factory in Paramount and is now on display at the Hockey Hall of Fame in Toronto. Lelo Grasso operated No. 21 and was well-known for his "tip of the hat" as he entered and exited the ice.

continued from page 107

Zamboni drivers grew impatient with these slow patterns and resolved to emblazon a new path.

The hockey world stood aghast as the Minnesota North Stars took the bold step of introducing two Zamboni machines to resurface the ice. Drivers Mark Rasmussen and Bruce Tharaldson halved the time to clear the rink inside the North Stars' home at Met Center in Bloomington. The fans perched on the edges of their seats, awaiting a low-speed Zamboni crash that never materialized. "We ended up getting a newer Zamboni, so we had two of them," explains retired Zamboni driver Ed Chayer, who preceded the daring Rasmussen and Tharaldson on the North Stars' home ice. "I think it was kind of neat. They basically followed each other on opposite sides of the rink. I think they did it so they had more ice time." Today, dueling Zambonis are standard at all pro hockey games, reducing ice resurfacing to 6 to 8 minutes, and allowing more time for between-period shenanigans.

Don't Drink and Drive a Zamboni!

Driving the Zamboni may not require the same lightning reflexes of a goalie, but in 2005 a couple of deviants failed the

Boston Bruins' Machines

The refurbished Boston Bruins' Model E No. 21 stands next to a brand-new Zamboni 500 in front of the factory in Paramount.

Zamboni drivers' sacred oath to perfect ice. A driver at the Mennen Sports Arena in Morristown, New Jersey, was famously arrested that summer for speeding and driving a Zamboni while drunk. Officials were stumped. Was this a crime? After all, a driver's license generally isn't required to operate a Zamboni.

A few weeks later on August 12, 2005, another Zamboni driver at the Pavillon Jean Béliveau in Victoriaville, Quebec, was booked with a blood-alcohol level nearly four times the legal limit. "It's typically Canuck," commented Canadian prosecutor, Jean-François Royer as he fined the driver $1,350 in Canadian currency. As in the New Jersey case, police were confused whether driving a Zamboni while drunk was truly against the law. Researchers consulted the Canadian Criminal Code and the Zamboni was determined to be a motorized vehicle, operators of which mustn't be inebriated.

"Higher than that and there's a danger of coma," prosecutor Royer told Toronto's *National Post*, in reference to the driver's blood-alcohol level. The driver's license was suspended for a year. Later the same evening, he was pulled over while driving home from the arena. He refused a Breathalyzer test, but somehow talked his way out of a DUI. The errant Zamboni maneuvers earlier in the evening stuck on his record, however.

When asked his opinion of drunken Zamboni drivers, Richard Zamboni just shakes his head and advises, "Don't drink and operate any machinery."

Zamboni Reverence vs. Blasphemy

While visionary artists have used Zamboni machines as their muse—and sometimes as their canvas—the Zamboni Company has brainstormed creative Zamboni merchandise. Miniature

In the Land of the Midnight Sun

No, these Zamboni ice resurfacers aren't racing for the Norwegian audience—they're keeping the oval slick for speed skaters at the 1994 winter games in Lillehammer.

ZAMBONI

Runaway Zamboni!

Ed Chayer drove the Zamboni ice resurfacer at the Met Center for the Minnesota North Stars from March 1969 to May 1992. Most events went off without a hitch. "I was there 23 years," he says. "I probably drove the Zamboni for every event, including Ice Follies, for 15 years."

Then one evening, with a full house for a playoff game, his Zamboni went out of control. "I was clearing the ice when the throttle cable fell off the pulley underneath the dashboard," Ed explains. "The engine stayed wide open and I was barreling towards the boards. I tried to shut off the ignition, but I couldn't stop. The people in the stands next to the boards were watching me nervously. I was left helpless out there with a runaway Zamboni. I'm getting closer and closer and they're starting to stand up and run away. I tried to make the turn, but back in those days, there were no studded tires on Zambonis. I went sliding sideways and smashed into the boards. Bang!"

The Zamboni stopped, Ed recovered from the shock, and then restarted it. "I tried to get it off the ice with it roaring, so we could lift the bucket up and dump the snow." The throttle cable was easily fixed and the Zamboni was ready to clear the ice after the next period.

Zamboni toys have been manufactured with every NHL team logo and with many college team colors. Finally, fans can drive their own mini radio-controlled Zamboni. In February 2005, McDonald's restaurants offered a very special treat in their Canadian Happy Meals: a mini plastic Zamboni ice resurfacer. McDonald's in the United States didn't offer the same prize, making the little Zamboni toys an instant collectible south of the border.

Other Zamboni merchandise has included license plate holders ("My other car is a Zamboni") and Beanie Babies ("Zambeanie Babies"). And the tension around the Monopoly board erupted when the age-old battle over the little pewter shoe, top hat, and dog was complicated by the addition of a Zamboni game piece.

Most popular of all Zamboni objects, however, are T-shirts that are silk-screened with the company logo and sold in ice arenas in 3/4-scale Zamboni-shaped kiosks. Lindsay Chaney in *Business Monday Report* wrote, "Some of the clothing is narrowly targeted, for example, bald men with grandchildren. A child's shirt has a caption that reads: 'Ice as slick as your grandpa's head.'"

All this Zamboni reverence isn't universal, however. Italians easily recognize the name as one of their own but often seem confused by the veneration bestowed these hulky machines by the Canadians and Americans. And at the 2006 Winter Olympics in Torino, Italy, Mats Olsson, the media officer for the eventual gold medal–winning Swedish men's hockey team, was asked his opinion of Zamboni ice resurfacers. "This is a very American question," he responded. "We are very different people and we don't accord any high status to these machines. I don't know anyone who cares who cleans the ice."

Frank Zamboni's mother was born just 19 miles (31 kilometers) away from where the 2006 Winter Olympics were held, so it should have been a long-awaited homecoming when 16 Zamboni machines cleared the ice in Torino. However, Alessandro Tancredi, a fan for Team Italia wearing a bright blue-and-white wig told *Bloomberg News*, "I've heard that [Zamboni ice resurfacers] are a

Pride of Canada

A Zamboni Model 520 made at the nearby Zamboni factory in Brantford, Ontario, poses on a seasonal outdoor rink in downtown Toronto.

INTERNATIONAL
RINKMANSHIP!
ZAMBONI

Across the Pond

This period advertisement trumpets the Zamboni company's inroads to international markets.

big deal in North America, but here, no. Here they just clean the ice." *Bloomberg News* also noted that "In Europe, even countries with more developed hockey cultures than Italy don't get the Zamboni cult."

Snoopy Clears the Ice

Perhaps the biggest Zamboni zealot was Charles Schulz, creator of the *Peanuts* comic strip. Schulz left his hometown of St. Paul for the greener pastures of Santa Rosa, California. Charlie Brown and the gang stayed in Minnesota, however, with ice rinks aplenty as the backdrop for the comic strip.

Perhaps missing all the outdoor winter rinks of the frozen north, Schulz had a private rink built near his home and bought his very own Zamboni ice resurfacer in 1968. To thank his new hometown of Santa Rosa, he gave the community their own indoor ice arena with its very own Zamboni.

Schulz's usage of a Zamboni as the punch line in many *Peanuts* strips popularized the ice resurfacer like no big-budget ad campaign could ever have done. "I'll never forget. It was 1980," Richard Zamboni recalls. "We were on our way back from the Olympics and I got a call from a friend at the *L.A. Times*. He said, 'Did you see *Peanuts* today?' And I said no. He

said, 'Zamboni is mentioned in the cartoon strip.'"

Charles Schulz met Richard Zamboni and told him that after Snoopy drove the Zamboni, Californians would come up to him and ask, "What the heck is a Zamboni?"

Over the years, 48 references were made to Zamboni in *Peanuts*, including one strip on the baseball diamond in which Charlie Brown yells to Lucy, who is dozing in the outfield, "In case you're interested, there's a Zamboni headed your way."

Racing Zambonis on Prime Time

Zamboni not only made it into *Webster's Dictionary* but somehow managed to sneak into the lexicon of those with their fingers on the pulse of pop culture. Alex Trebek, a Canadian, used the famous ice resurfacer on *Jeopardy* as the answer to a question—or rather a question to an answer.

A Zamboni helped solve a murder on *CSI* in which the investigator pronounced, "I love a Zamboni."

"We all do," agreed his sidekick.

"The thing I love about Zamboni is they pick up everything." Including the forensic clues needed to crack the *CSI* mystery.

During one Winter Olympics, Jay Leno showed off his favorite Olympic souvenir, an "Olympic Zamboni Ice Maker! This is the hit of the party—who doesn't love crushed ice?"

THIS BRILLIANT PERFORMER SOLVES CE MAKING PROBLEMS FOR GOOD...

THIS WORLD FAMOUS INVENTION RE-SURFACES THE ICE WITH A MIRROR-LIKE FINISH IN A FRACTION OF THE TIME USED BY PREVIOUS METHODS.

When he revved up the mini Zamboni, ice flew all over the *Tonight Show* stage.

David Letterman was close behind Leno when he read his "Top 10 List of Rejected Olympic Sports" that listed "Four Man Zamboni" near the top.

For the 1998 Winter Olympics in Nagano, Japan, Letterman had the brilliant idea of racing two Zamboni machines down 53rd Street in New York City. Tim Mann worked for the *Late Show* and remembers getting the call from Letterman to find two Zamboni machines to race. "I had a couple of days lead on this, so I talked to the factory in Canada," says Mann. "They were excited about it but couldn't help me, so they sent me a turtleneck with a Z on the neck."

Anything can be found in Manhattan for the right price. Letterman paid to rent a flatbed truck to haul in a Zamboni from a small community in New Jersey, and another machine was trucked to Midtown from Madison Square Garden. "Since the [New York] Rangers were out of town, we could get it," Mann remembers.

Then Mann was left with the problem of how to convince the city of New York that racing two Zamboni ice resurfacers down 53rd Street at 5 p.m. was a good idea. "The funny thing is that the mayor's office for TV and film that gave permission is actually in

Bye-Bye, Zamboni

A brand-new Zamboni ice resurfacer navigates the streets of Paramount, California, after a spin at Iceland Skating Rink for a test run. ***Peter Read Miller***

the building" says Mann. "It was really convenient for us to just go downstairs and get permission. These guys were basically film cops—they don't cover a beat, they basically block off traffic."

Two employees, Mujibar and Sirajul, from K&L's Rock America souvenir shop next to the Ed Sullivan Theater in which the *Late Show* is taped were chosen as the drivers. Had they ever driven a Zamboni resurfacer before back home in India? "No way, they hadn't done anything like this before," Mann says. "They had probably never even seen a Zamboni before."

The *Late Show* is filmed at 5 p.m., exactly the same time everyone in the city is trying desperately to drive home. With the help of New York's finest, cars, yellow taxis, and buses were gridlocked for miles while Letterman played the joke of having two Zamboni ice resurfacers race at a snail's pace. Fortunately for the motorists, the resurfacers weren't laying down ice.

"Midtown was a total debacle," Mann continues. Traffic was stopped and Mann waited with the two Zamboni machines until Letterman was ready to race. Mann gazed at the stopped traffic for miles. "Look at the mess we're making!" Mann remembers saying. In keeping with the bizarre but catchy humor of David Letterman, Mann confesses that "Ultimately it was underwhelming for everyone. The idea was better than reality, but at least we can brag about it now!"

Who knows what other Zamboni feats lay in store? An around-the-world tour? Keeping Greenland's glaciers from melting? The name "Zamboni" has brought smiles to even the most hardened hockey fans, inspired artists, and Olympic champions, and provided the pause that refreshes after breath-taking triple axles and betwixt fast-paced periods of knock-'em-up hockey. Mesmerizing fans for more than fifty years, Zamboni is on a roll into the new millennium.

Timeline

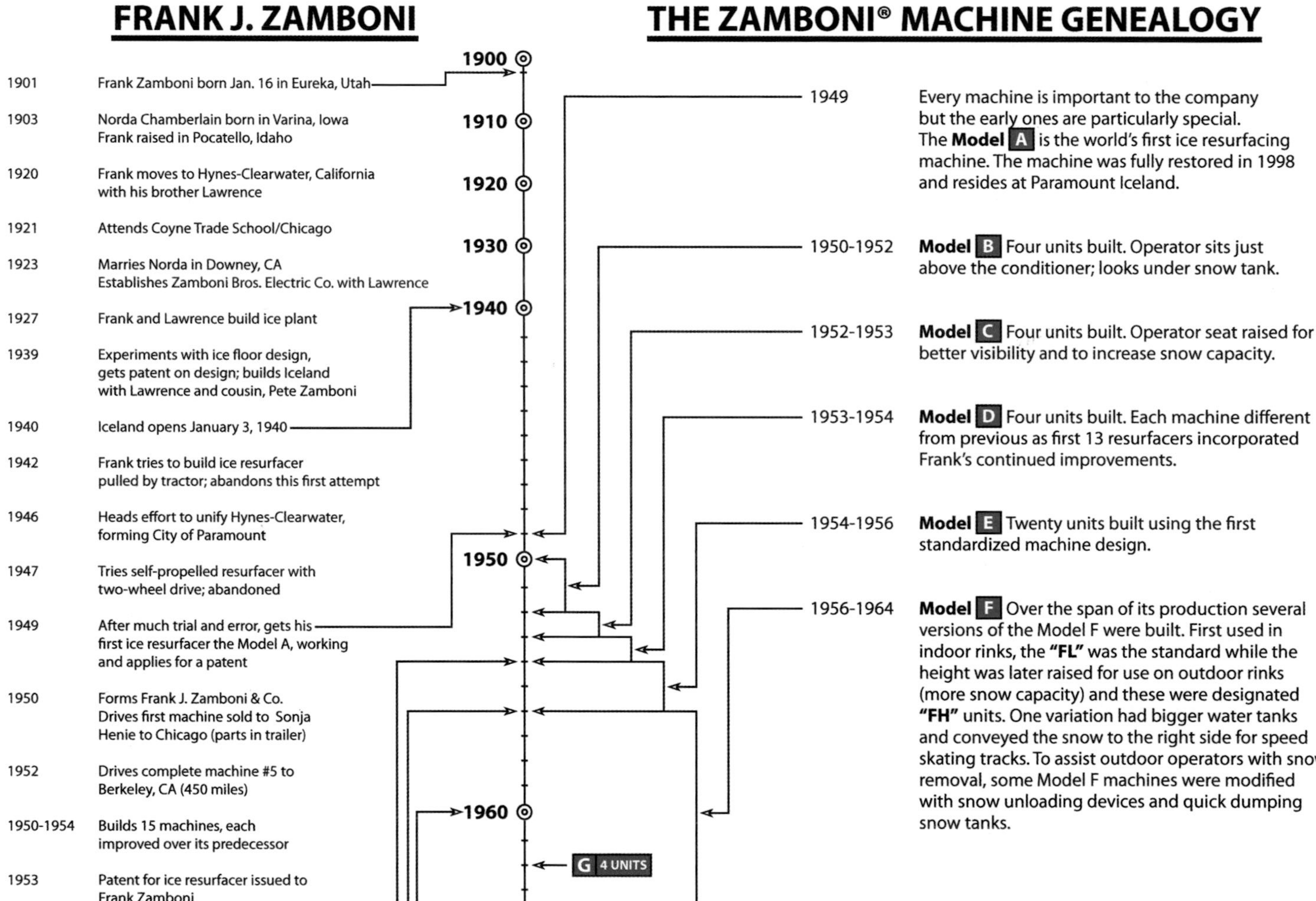

FRANK J. ZAMBONI
THE ZAMBONI® MACHINE GENEALOGY
1900
1910
1920
1930
1940
1950
1960
1901 Frank Zamboni born Jan. 16 in Eureka, Utah
1903 Norda Chamberlain born in Varina, Iowa
Frank raised in Pocatello, Idaho
1920 Frank moves to Hynes-Clearwater, California
with his brother Lawrence
1921 Attends Coyne Trade School/Chicago
1923 Marries Norda in Downey, CA
Establishes Zamboni Bros. Electric Co. with Lawrence
1927 Frank and Lawrence build ice plant
1939 Experiments with ice floor design,
gets patent on design; builds Iceland
with Lawrence and cousin, Pete Zamboni
1940 Iceland opens January 3, 1940
1942 Frank tries to build ice resurfacer
pulled by tractor; abandons this first attempt
1946 Heads effort to unify Hynes-Clearwater,
forming City of Paramount
1947 Tries self-propelled resurfacer with
two-wheel drive; abandoned
1949 After much trial and error, gets his
first ice resurfacer the Model A, working
and applies for a patent
1950 Forms Frank J. Zamboni & Co.
Drives first machine sold to Sonja
Henie to Chicago (parts in trailer)
1952 Drives complete machine #5 to
Berkeley, CA (450 miles)
1950-1954 Builds 15 machines, each
improved over its predecessor
1953 Patent for ice resurfacer issued to
Frank Zamboni
1949 Every machine is important to the company
but the early ones are particularly special.
The Model A is the world's first ice resurfacing
machine. The machine was fully restored in 1998
and resides at Paramount Iceland.
1950-1952 Model B Four units built. Operator sits just
above the conditioner; looks under snow tank.
1952-1953 Model C Four units built. Operator seat raised for
better visibility and to increase snow capacity.
1953-1954 Model D Four units built. Each machine different
from previous as first 13 resurfacers incorporated
Frank's continued improvements.
1954-1956 Model E Twenty units built using the first
standardized machine design.
1956-1964 Model F Over the span of its production several
versions of the Model F were built. First used in
indoor rinks, the "FL" was the standard while the
height was later raised for use on outdoor rinks
(more snow capacity) and these were designated
"FH" units. One variation had bigger water tanks
and conveyed the snow to the right side for speed
skating tracks. To assist outdoor operators with snow
removal, some Model F machines were modified
with snow unloading devices and quick dumping
snow tanks.
G 4 UNITS

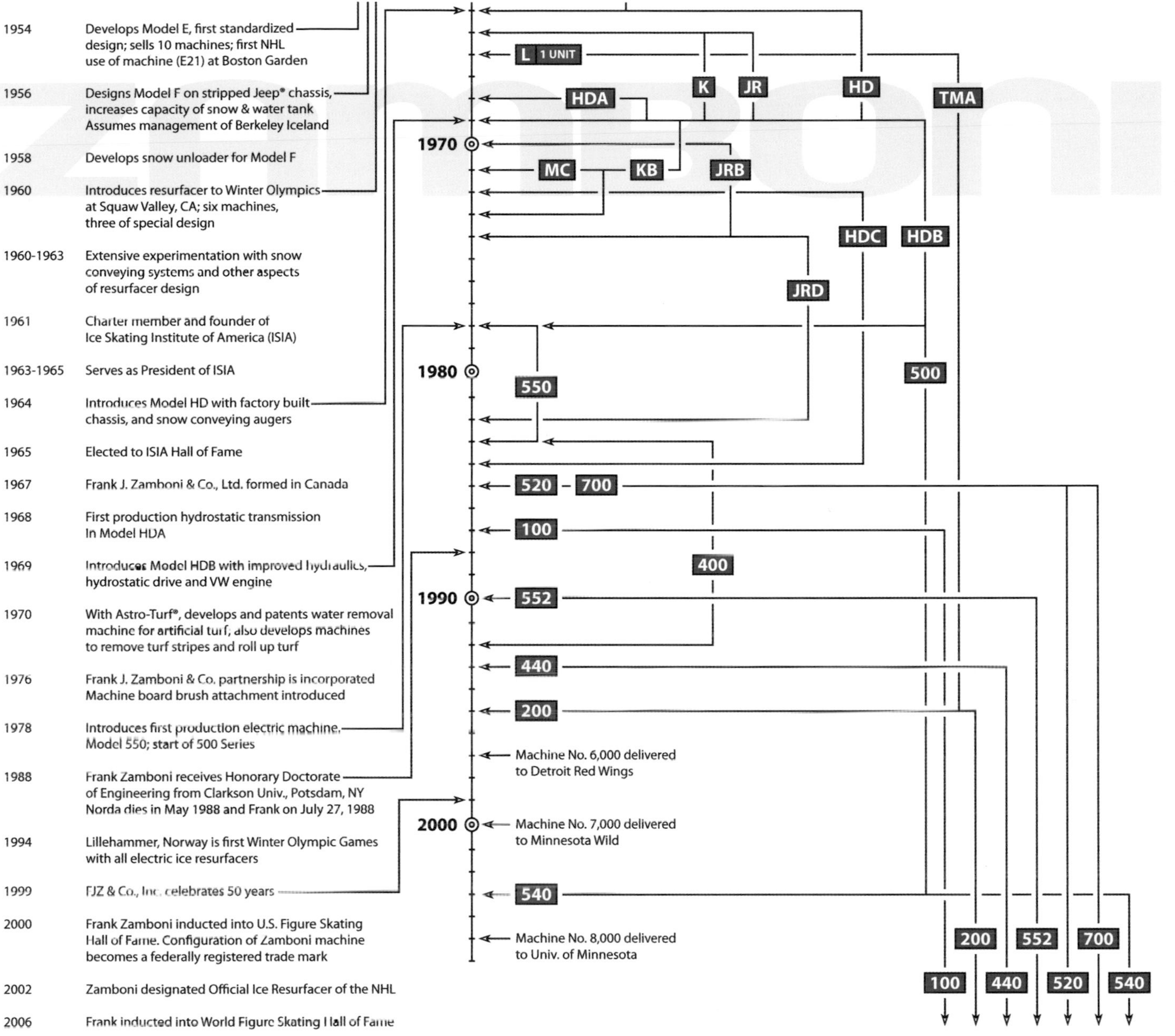

1954 Develops Model E, first standardized design; sells 10 machines; first NHL use of machine (E21) at Boston Garden
1956 Designs Model F on stripped Jeep® chassis, increases capacity of snow & water tank
Assumes management of Berkeley Iceland
1958 Develops snow unloader for Model F
1960 Introduces resurfacer to Winter Olympics at Squaw Valley, CA; six machines, three of special design
1960-1963 Extensive experimentation with snow conveying systems and other aspects of resurfacer design
1961 Charter member and founder of Ice Skating Institute of America (ISIA)
1963-1965 Serves as President of ISIA
1964 Introduces Model HD with factory built chassis, and snow conveying augers
1965 Elected to ISIA Hall of Fame
1967 Frank J. Zamboni & Co., Ltd. formed in Canada
1968 First production hydrostatic transmission In Model HDA
1969 Introduces Model HDB with improved hydraulics, hydrostatic drive and VW engine
1970 With Astro-Turf®, develops and patents water removal machine for artificial turf, also develops machines to remove turf stripes and roll up turf
1976 Frank J. Zamboni & Co. partnership is incorporated
Machine board brush attachment introduced
1978 Introduces first production electric machine, Model 550; start of 500 Series
1988 Frank Zamboni receives Honorary Doctorate of Engineering from Clarkson Univ., Potsdam, NY
Norda dies in May 1988 and Frank on July 27, 1988
1994 Lillehammer, Norway is first Winter Olympic Games with all electric ice resurfacers
1999 FJZ & Co., Inc. celebrates 50 years
2000 Frank Zamboni inducted into U.S. Figure Skating Hall of Fame. Configuration of Zamboni machine becomes a federally registered trade mark
2002 Zamboni designated Official Ice Resurfacer of the NHL
2006 Frank inducted into World Figure Skating Hall of Fame
1970
1980
1990
2000
L 1 UNIT
K
JR
HD
TMA
HDA
MC
KB
JRB
HDC
HDB
JRD
550
500
520
700
100
400
552
440
200
Machine No. 6,000 delivered to Detroit Red Wings
Machine No. 7,000 delivered to Minnesota Wild
540
Machine No. 8,000 delivered to Univ. of Minnesota
200
552
700
100
440
520
540
ZAMBONI®

Appendix
The Early Zamboni Models

Unit	Model	Delivered	Purchased by	Fate
n/a	A	1949	Iceland, Paramount, CA	Restored in 1998; on display at Iceland.
No. 1	B	1950	Pasadena Winter Garden	Dismantled
No. 2	B	1950	Arthur Wirtz/Sonja Henie Ice Revue	Unknown
No. 3	B	1951	Sonja Henie Ice Revue	Unknown
No. 4	B	1952	Ice Capades	Restored 1974; now in U.S. Hockey Hall of Fame, Eveleth, MN.
No. 5	C	1952	Iceland, Berkeley, CA	Dismantled
No. 6	C	1953	Iceland, Paramount, CA	Converted to Model F
No. 7	C	1953	Chicago Arena	Unknown
No. 8	C	1953	Sonja Henie Ice Revue	Dismantled in Europe
No. 9	—	———	Serial number not used	
No. 10	C	1953	Sutro's, San Francisco, CA	Unknown
No. 11	C	1953	Denver University	Unknown
No. 12	D	1953	Holiday on Ice Show	Unknown
No. 13	—	———	Serial number not used	
No. 14	D	1953	Philadelphia Skating Club	Dismantled
No. 15	D	1954	Pasadena Winter Garden	Dismantled
No. 16	E	1954	Ice Capades	Unknown
No. 17	E	1954	Laval, PQ, Sports Center	Unknown; first Zamboni machine in Canada.
No. 18	E	1954	Dallas State Fair	Unknown
No. 19	E	1954	Lynn, MA, Sports Center	Unknown
No. 20	E	1954	Boston Arena	Unknown
No. 21	E	1954	Boston Garden	Restored; first Zamboni machine in NHL now in the Hockey Hall of Fame, Toronto, ON.

No. 22	E	1954	Providence, RI, Hockey Club	Unknown
No. 23	E	1954	Philadelphia Arena	Unknown
No. 24	E	1954	Ice Capades, Pittsburgh, PA	Unknown
No. 25	E	1954	Cleveland Skating Club	Dismantled
No. 26	E	1954	Hershey, PA, Arena	Unknown
No. 27	E	1954	Casino Skating Palace Boardwalk, Asbury Park, NJ	Unknown
No. 28	E	1954	Rensselaer Polytechnic Institute, Troy, NY	Unknown
No. 29	E	1955	Montreal Forum	First Zamboni machine used by a Canadian NHL team.
No. 30	E	1955	City of Verdun, PQ	Unknown
No. 31	E	1955	Rochester, NY, Institute of Technology	Unknown
No. 32	E	1955	City of Rochester, NY	Unknown
No. 33	E	1955	Michael Kirby Ice Skating School, River Forest, IL	Unknown
No. 34	E	1955	Tower Cabana Skating Rink, Chicago, IL	Restored
No. 35	E	1956	Ice Palace, Norfolk, VA	Unknown
No. 36	E	1956	Beaver Dam, NY, Winter Club	Being restored by Zamboni
No. 37	F	1956	St. Paul, MN, Auditorium	First Model F; on display at Xcel Energy Center, St. Paul, MN.

Index